CHRISTIAN ENCOUNTERS

JANE
AUSTEN

D0048653

CHRISTIAN ENCOUNTERS

JANE AUSTEN

PETER LEITHART

Thomas Nelson
Since 1798

NASHVILLE   DALLAS   MEXICO CITY   RIO DE JANEIRO

Published in Nashville, Tennessee, by Thomas Nelson. Thomas Nelson is a registered trademark of Thomas Nelson, Inc.

Thomas Nelson, Inc. titles may be purchased in bulk for educational, business, fund-raising, or sales promotional use. For information, please e-mail SpecialMarkets@ThomasNelson.com.

Library of Congress Cataloging-in-Publication Data [to come]

ISBN: 978-1-59555-302-7

Printed in the United States of America

09 10 11 12 HCI 6 5 4 3 2 1

CONTENTS

INTRODUCTION: JANEIA

> "She was like a child— quite a child very lively and
> fully of humor— most amiable— most beloved."
>
> —FULWAR WILLIAM FOWLE, on Jane Austen

Neither Jane Austen nor her family could leave her characters alone. Her nephew James Edward Austen-Leigh and niece Anna Lefroy frequently asked what happened after the novels ended, and Aunt Jane would oblige with many little particulars about the subsequent career of some of her people. In this traditionary way we learned that Miss Steele never succeeded in catching the Doctor; that Kitty Bennet was satisfactorily married to a clergyman near Pemberly, while Mary obtained nothing higher than one of her uncle Philips' clerks, and was content to be considered a star in the society of Meryton; that the "considerable sum" given by Mrs. Norris to William Price was one pound; that Mr Woodhouse survived his daughter's marriage, and kept her and Mr Knightley

from settling at Donwell, about two years; and that the letters placed by Frank Churchill before Jane Fairfax, which she
swept away unread, contained the word "pardon."[1]

We can't leave Jane's characters alone either. Drop in at
the nearest big-box bookstore, and you will find shelves stuffed
with prequels and sequels and every other kind of "-quel" imag-
inable. Over there is Emma Tennant's *An Unequal Marriage:
Pride and Prejudice Twenty Years Later*, in which Fitzwilliam has
reverted back to his haughty pre-Elizabethan self, his son has
married a barmaid, and his steward pines for his wife. Down
the shelf is Linda Berdoll's *The Bar Sinister: Pride and Prejudice
Continues*, which gives details of the Darcys' sex life and intro-
duces a young workman at Pemberley who is reputed to be
Darcy's illegitimate son and who stands, due to Elizabeth's bar-
renness, to inherit his fortune. Turn the corner and you'll find
Bridget Jones's Diary, by Helen Fielding, less a sequel than a
modern retelling of *Pride and Prejudice*, complete with Mark
Darcy, an apparent descendant of Austen's character Mr. Darcy.
Then there's S. N. Dyer's *Resolve and Resistance*, in which
Elizabeth uses "Pemberly as the base for a guerilla movement
against Napoleon's occupying army" and learns "with the help
of Admiral Nelson, to navigate a fleet of hot-air balloons . . . so
as to lead this English resistance to victory."[2] If "over the top"
is where you live, you might check out *Pride and Prejudice and
Zombies*, billed as an updating of the "classic Regency romance"
enhanced by "ultraviolent zombie mayhem."

Though *Pride and Prejudice* is far and away the most often
exploited of Austen's books, there are similar novels based on

Emma, Mansfield Park, Sense and Sensibility, not to mention Stephanie Barron's Jane Austen Mysteries, in which Austen herself turns sleuth. I imagine someone somewhere is sweating away over a manuscript in which the intrepid and reincarnated Lizzie leads British special forces through the wastes of Afghanistan to the cave where Osama bin Laden makes his headquarters.

Time would fail were I to list the film and television productions of Austen's novels, many of which hastily capitalize on the astonishing success of Sue Birtwistle's 1995 adaptation of *Pride and Prejudice*.[3] From Hollywood to Bollywood, from ANE to BBC and on through the media alphabet, producers can't resist the costumed dramatics of an Austen adaptation, which can be both sexy and staid, both popular and elevating. Few of these succeed as reproductions of Austen's novels. The camera can only record surfaces, but the whole point of an Austen novel is to record the ironic discrepancies between surface and reality, to expose social masks as masks. As literary critic Roger Sales cleverly put it, Austen adaptations are filmed as if Mr. Collins held the camera, lingering lovingly over the Regency finery—the china and the delicate teacups and the always-groaning sideboard.[4]

Some of the best Austen films are not Austen films at all, but more distant adaptations, like Whit Stillman's wonderfully Austenesque *Metropolitan*. Stillman's talky films work because he doesn't attempt to reproduce Regency England, with its connotations of elegance and craftsmanship; rather, he discovers contemporary or near-contemporary social settings (in *Metropolitan*, the haute bourgeoisie of New York City "not so long ago") into which he can plop a plot. The failure to provide the right social setting is the main flaw in the otherwise charming *Emma* adaptation, *Clueless*. Southern California is many things, but a rigidly hierarchical society it ain't. Emma Woodhouse was perhaps the first of the Valley Girls, but *Emma* becomes ludicrous unless its romance develops against the background of a fixed social structure.

We can't even leave poor Jane herself alone. Biographers (*mea culpa*) pore over her letters, which her sister Cassandra wanted to destroy or hide or keep to herself and the family circle. Tourists stomp through Jane's various homes, and Hollywood has produced a film about her life, dressing it up with fictional characters and situations to work the germ of a romance into a two-hour feature. *Becoming Jane* (2007) is based on a biography by Jon Spence, which, despite many virtues, operates on the silly premise that Austen drew everything she wrote more or less directly from life. Spence treats Austen's youthful writings (known as her *Juvenalia*) and the novels as autobiographical allegories, and the film takes this much further, assuming that Jane could not have written what she did not experience. She could not have imagined an elopement without eloping, could not vividly depict a girl falling in love with a rake unless she had had an affair herself, could not show Elizabeth Bennet skewering a rich suitor unless she had been stalked by a large clumsy booby, could not *invent* a Lady Catherine. Not even Spence was bold enough to create a romance with a nonexistent "Mr. Wisley." One might as well ask, was Agatha Christie a murderess?

Whether Austen pined after Tom Lefroy, as Spence and the film suggest, is open to debate. But we can be morally certain that the young woman who wrote *Pride and Prejudice* never acted like

Lydia, and that the woman who wrote *Northanger Abbey* would have been self-aware enough to stop short of making her own life a breathless romance. The film is endurable only if we imagine how heartily Jane Austen would have laughed at it.

Austen has become what she never was in life, what she would have been horrified to be: a literary celebrity. But why should a seventeenth-century spinster novelist become a celebrity? Why is there not a similar enthusiasm for Dickens or Trollope or one of the Brontës?

Some of the reasons are inherent in Austen's books themselves. Austen strove for accuracy in detail, but she refrained from writing topical novels. The closest she gets to entering a contemporary debate is in the discussions of ordination, pluralism, and the public role of a pastor in *Mansfield Park*, but this issue hardly enflames twenty-first-century readers. As Claire Harman puts it, since Austen "knew that pinning her works to a particular time would date them," she "unpinned" them.[5] Her difficulty getting her work published is also an important factor here. Austen rewrote her early novels again and again, and realized that with the passage of time the earlier works had become obsolete. To make her early works useful, she minimized contemporary references,[6] and this lends Austen's novels a timelessness that makes them perennially appealing.

Nostalgia plays a role as well. British soldiers took Austen to the trenches in World War I, a fact documented by Rudyard Kipling's "The Janeites," written when Kipling was being soothed by Austen while recovering from a stomach operation on the Riviera.[7] On his way to meet with Roosevelt and Stalin in 1943, Winston Churchill, exhausted and bedridden with pneumonia, found solace in *Pride and Prejudice*. "What calm lives they had, these people!" he remarked.[8]

A more significant answer is that Austen and her work have been caught up in celebrity culture. *Pride and Prejudice* was a television hit and made Colin Firth a sexy star, most famous for the diving scene that appears nowhere in Austen's book, and the 1995 film *Sense and Sensibility* won multiple awards, including an Oscar for Emma Thompson's screenplay. Pop culture likes nothing better than a sequel, and so producers keep churning out the remakes. Repetitive as they are, Austen's novels are peculiarly suited to the industry. There is a built-in sameness with variation that Hollywood loves. Sucked into celebrity culture, further, Austen has become a public domain brand name, detachable from her actual books and capable of transforming anything she touches.[9] Depictions of mousy Fanny Price in recent film adaptations of *Mansfield Park* bear little resemblance to Austen's character, but watching Billie Piper as Fanny gives viewers the satisfactions of "high art" and pop celebrity in a single show.

The current obsession with everything Austen might be taken as a form of dementia. More plausibly, it is a secular religion. The novelist and critic E. M. Forster already recognized the religious dimensions of the mania for all things Austen that I call "Janeia," calling himself a "Jane Austenite" who, "like all regular church-goers . . . scarcely notices what is being said."[10] It was already an established faith. When stained-glass figures were added to the Winchester Cathedral in 1900, there was a portrait of Augustine, who, the guidebook helpfully mentioned, is also known as "St. Austin." The cult has its pilgrimages (to Steventon, where no rectory survives, to Bath, Chawton, and everywhere else Austen stepped) and its relics (including a clipping of hair bought at auction in 1946 and donated to the Chawton museum).

Characters in Karen Joy Fowler's *The Jane Austen Book Club* consult a Magic 8 Ball® filled with lines from Austen's novels as if it were an oracle, and Austen books and tours promise a monastic retreat into Regency stillness. For the faithful, it's not necessary to touch what Jane touched or walk where she walked. Sets and costumes used for Austen film adaptations are themselves sufficiently iconic.[11]

According to sociologist Christopher Rojek, celebrity in its contemporary form depends not only on the media, which puts celebrities in front of many more people more often than ever before, but also on "the democratization of society," "the decline in organized religion," and "the commodification of everyday life." For Rojek, "celebrities have filled the absence created by the decay in the popular belief in the divine right of kings, and the death of God." In a democratized society, which operates by the myth of the common man, celebrity offers an opportunity for distinction: "the dramatical personality and achieved style inscribe[s] distinction and grab[s] popular attention." Even the notorious become celebrities, because they stand out against the drab background of social indistinction.[12] In the absence of kings, celebrities are now the ones with "two bodies"—the mortal body that dies and the immortal, superhuman body of light up on the screen. "Janeiacs" likewise feel they have a personal intimacy with Austen, even though thousands share the same feeling.

The cult of Jane is nothing new, and has had as many devotees among biographers and historians as among novel readers. It started with her own family's memoirs of her life and character. It would be arrogant to dismiss her family's reminiscences, but their recollections are internally incoherent (supposedly, she never had a bad word to say about anyone, yet possessed an unerring sense of the ridiculous; and she combined all the perfections of all her best characters—Fanny Price *and* Elizabeth Bennet?!), and it is even more difficult to reconcile their accounts with the shrewd, clever, sometimes catty woman we come to know in the *Juvenalia*, novels, and letters. Austen's brother Henry started it with the brief sketch that prefaced the posthumously published *Northanger Abbey/Persuasion*, and nephew James Edward Austen-Leigh's 1870 memoir launched the first great wave of Janeia by smoothing the acerbic edges of his aunt's character and offering to the world a saccharine Jane who became a model of domesticity and femininity, a Victorian Madonna. It would only be a matter of time before someone—the American writer William Dean Howells, as it turned out—dubbed her "Divine Jane."[13]

Such adulation provokes readers and biographers to debunk, and not everyone has resisted the temptation. Howells's friend Mark Twain apparently couldn't stop reading Austen, but he despised her "Presbyterian" characters, expressed wonder that "they allowed her to die a natural death," and, delighted to discover a shipboard library without any Austen, concluded, "That one omission alone would make a fairly good library out of a library that hadn't a book in it."[14]

Every life is infinite. A life of Jane Austen cannot remain a life of Jane Austen, but becomes also about the life of her parents, her brothers and sister, her aunts and uncles and dozens of cousins, and her friends; the village where she was born; the town of Bath; the cottage in Chawton; Winchester, where she lived her last days; and the cathedral where she was buried. It is the life of eighteenth-century England, which clashes with the life of eighteenth-century France and America and India. And how can we understand anything about the eighteenth century without attention to the seventeenth, and the sixteenth, and so on back to the first fiat of the creation week?

Yet a biographer has to piece together this infinite life from the very finite shards and fragments that people leave behind. Austen left behind letters, six finished novels, a couple of unfinished ones, and some juvenile writing. At the various Janeite shrines one can find pieces of St. Jane's furniture and other relics she touched and used and thereby charged with her sacred energy. Paste all these pieces together, and you still don't have a full-length portrait, much less a three-dimensional figure. The attempt to recapture Jane Austen from these bits and pieces requires an act of imagination.

I am not of Howells; but neither am I of Twain. In the brief compass of this biography, I have tried to capture the varied sides of Austen's character. Early biographers often turned her into a model of Victorian Christian domestic femininity, and emphasized her Christian faith in an evangelical idiom she never used. In reaction, many more recent biographers all but ignore her faith. Both of those extremes distort Austen's life and character. I have tried to depict accurately the depth and sincerity of her Christianity, as well as her Anglican discomfort with religious emotion, but without losing sight of the other sides of her complex character—her playfulness, her satiric gift for ridicule, her "waspishness,"[15] her rigid morality. I have attempted to capture Jane Austen in full.

To my mind, no description quite captures all the dimensions of Austen as well as that of Fulwar William Fowle. Austen's life was intertwined with the Fowle family. Four of the Fowle boys were pupils of her father's, her sister Cassandra was engaged to Tom Fowle before his death in the West Indies, Austen herself admired Fulwar Fowle during their childhood so much that she predicted he would grow up to be secretary of state, and Charles Fowle was a particular friend of Jane's. All but one died prematurely; only Fulwar lived beyond young manhood. His oldest son, Fulwar William Fowle, knew Jane Austen when he was a boy and she in her twenties and thirties, and he recalled in 1838 that "she was pretty—certainly pretty—bright & a good deal of color in her face—like a doll." He immediately corrected himself: not a doll, "for she had so much expression"; rather, a "child."[16]

Fulwar meant this as a description of her appearance, but few have captured more of Austen's character in a single word. Austen grew from little Jenny to Miss Jane Austen to Aunt Jane to "a Lady" to "the author of *Sense & Sensibility*" to a pop culture phenomenon. But in life, and in her work, Austen retained many of the qualities she had as a child and young teenager. Childlikeness might not strike us as an apt description of a "serious" novelist like Austen, but this only highlights how pretentious we are about art and artists. Anyone who spends her life making up stories has got to have more than her fair share of whimsy, and nearly all Austen's virtues, personal and artistic, as well as nearly all of her vices, are those of a woman who, at the center of her soul, remained "Jenny Austen" all her life.

1

AUSTEN'S WORLD

J ane Austen's world was a world in upheaval. She was born nine months after the beginning of the American War of Independence, and during her girlhood the United States adopted the Constitution and French revolutionaries stormed the Bastille and later unleashed the Terror. As a young adult, she heard accounts of the Napoleonic Wars from her brothers, and watched as the entire British nation mobilized for war.[1] Britain was at war again in America when she was in her thirties, and in 1815, two years before she died, the Napoleonic era ended with the Treaty of Vienna.

A literary revolution matched the political one. The 1784 death of sage, poet, essayist, lexicographer, Christian moralist, and novelist Samuel Johnson marked the end of an era, and by the end of the next decade William Wordsworth and Samuel Taylor Coleridge had published *Lyrical Ballads*, a collection of poems with a famous preface that launched the Romantic movement in British poetry. The lives of the younger Romantic poets are almost contained within Austen's. Byron was born in

1788 and died fighting for Greek independence in 1824; Shelley lived from 1792 to 1822, and Keats from 1795 to 1821.

Though the Evangelical revivals of the early eighteenth century had cooled, a new burst of reforming zeal exploded during her lifetime. "Evangelicalism gradually strengthened within the Anglican fold, through the ministries of men like John Fletcher, Henry Venn and John Newton (Cowper's friend and collaborator). At the end of the century, William Wilberforce and the "Clapham Sect" gave fresh impetus to an Evangelical revival, which was later to have a profound effect on the private lives and public manners of the Victorians. These wealthy Anglicans believed that their faith should be reflected in good works. They led the campaign to abolish the slave trade, founded the British and Foreign Bible Society and supported missionary work at home and abroad."[2] The greatest achievement of this new wave of Evangelicalism was the abolition of the slave trade, achieved in 1807.

The first railroad did not begin operation until 1825, but already in Austen's lifetime the English cut a network of canals through the countryside, and several inventions—the flying shuttle, the spinning jenny, the power loom, and the cotton gin—made cheap pre-made fabric and clothing available for the first time. More people were able to buy more goods than ever before, and items once affordable only to the upper classes were available to middle and even lower classes. Rural women could follow the changing fashions of the city in fashion magazines and catalogues, and they could purchase fashionable goods in local shops.

Shopping was fast becoming a national pastime, particularly

in London and in elegant regional centers like Bath. By 1801, there were 74,500 shops in England, far more than any other European country, and the best shopping districts of London foreshadowed today's malls: "Oxford Street in particular was very smart, brilliantly lit with oil lamps, its shops staying open until ten o'clock at night. All sorts of attractive goods were enticingly displayed in bright bow-fronted windows, and more were laid out for inspection in the spacious first-floor showrooms of some of the larger establishments."[3] England was what economist Adam Smith had called it, a "nation of shop-keepers."

Austen's life was touched by these revolutions at several points. Her cousin Eliza's husband died at the guillotine; she shopped in London, lived in Bath, and, observant as she was, couldn't help but notice that a new world was emerging. Yet for practical purposes, Austen's world, and especially her initial world, was a good deal smaller.

Jenny Austen was born on December 16, 1775, in the parish rectory at Stevenson, a small village in the Hampshire Downs, during a winter so severe that her parents could not take her to the village church for a public christening until the following April. Steventon lay in an angle formed by two roads, the northern one running from London to the West Countries and the southern from London to Winchester. Her first home was a modestly improved two-story brick structure, with two kitchens, a study in the older back part of the house for Jane's father, seven bedrooms, and three attics. In the enclosed garden behind, set off by a row of spruce fir, were cherry and other fruit trees. One gate of the garden led to a pathway under the cover of elms, the "Wood Walk," and at the other end of the garden was a gate that opened onto a lane leading toward the Tudor-era Steventon Manor House, where the Digweed family lived. Up the hill from the Manor was the village church, first built in the eleventh century, and near the church grew a yew tree reputed to be as old as the building. Near the Wood Walk gate was a tall white pole with a weathercock, which made a "scrooping sound" as the wind turned it. In the spring, the aroma of honeysuckle that twined around the pole filled the garden.[4]

As a girl, Jane often visited the rectory in Deane, a short walk north of Steventon, where her friends Martha and Mary Lloyd lived with their widowed mother from 1789 to 1792. To the south, a track led from Steventon to the London-Winchester Road, where, at the Wheatsheaf Inn, the stagecoach stopped twice daily to deliver mail. When the Lloyds moved to Ibthorpe House, nearly twenty miles to the northwest of Steventon, Jane continued her friendship, visiting their "early Georgian small house, of rosy chequered brickwork, with a hipped roof, dainty dentil frieze, perfectly proportioned sash-windows and a scrolled canopy over the central door." There, everything was "neatness, elegance, and comfort."[5] At nearby Manydown Park, Jane and her sister Cassandra visited Catherine and Elizabeth Bigg. Manydown was a "much grander place than Ibthorpe House, with a sweeping staircase of delicate ironwork ascending to a noble first-floor reception room lit by a large bay window."[6]

Austen's world was a world of chalk hills cut by slow-flowing streams and dotted with sheep; of fields filled with wheat and barley, turnips, peas, and beans; of meadows green with hay and clover and cut by hedgerows and forests of oak, beech, ash, and elm. Hampshire has few of the dramatic landscapes of the Lake

District or the Low Countries of Scotland. Yet Austen loved the natural beauties of Hampshire, and was attached to her home and village. But she was always most enchanted by people. When Austen was born, there were some thirty families in the parish,[7] but her closest neighbors were her immediate family. Fortunately for little Jenny Austen, that family was enchanting indeed.

A PROFOUND SCHOLAR

Since the Romantic period, artists have often been pictured as strangers to their surroundings, bohemian rebels against their social worlds, isolated geniuses who live in such a state of heightened alertness that they neglect, and can be forgiven for neglecting, quotidian niceties like mouthwash and deodorant. If they have a social set at all, it is the anti-social social set of similarly alienated artists. Jane Austen grew to be a literary genius of the first order, but she shows no signs of alienation or estrangement. She knew few other writers, and none well, and spent no time in urban literary circles. Throughout her life, her main social set was her family.

Fortunately for her, few families could have been more suited to encouraging Jane's particular talents than the Austens of Steventon. A comfortable though not wealthy middle gentry family, they shared the patriotic Tory prejudices, ambitions, and inclinations of their class, with one notable difference: they were an exceptionally literate, clever, witty, jovial, affectionate, and accomplished family. They were amused by the world around them, and often laughed at it. Early on, Jenny learned to do the same. It was a family Jenny could love, and admire.

George Austen (1731–1805), Jane's father, was the second child and first son of William Austen (1701–1737), a surgeon of Tonbridge descended from Kentish clothiers.[8] His mother was Rebecca Walter Austen, the widow of William Walter. When Rebecca Walter married William Austen, she already had a son of her own, William Hampson Walter. Together, William and Rebecca had three children, but Rebecca died in 1732, soon after giving birth to a daughter, Leonora, George's youngest sister. William Austen remarried Susanna Kelk in 1735, but eighteen months later, William died. Because of an oversight in his will, his wife had no legal obligation to provide anything for her stepchildren, George, and his sisters. Accordingly, she did *not* provide anything for her stepchildren, and the fortunes of George, his older sister Philadelphia, and his younger sister Leonora, were left to others.[9]

Philadelphia Austen (1730–1792), the most adventurous of the three, set off for India at the age of twenty-two aboard the *Bombay Castle*. If, as seems likely, her aim was to secure a husband in the colony, she succeeded. By February 1753, she was married to Tysoe Saul Hancock, a surgeon in Fort St. David, an outpost of the East India Company; and in 1761 they had their only child, Elizabeth, Jenny's cousin, whom everyone called "Eliza."[10] Hancock was not a successful man. He brought his wife and daughter back to England, but returned to India in 1768 to pursue various business ventures, none of which took off. He remained in India, sending missives exhorting his wife to provide a suitable education to their daughter and shipping back ingredients for curries, pickled mangoes and limes, and textile goods, some of which doubtless ended up in the possession of Jane Austen's family. Hancock died, a failed man, in Calcutta in November 1775, a month before Jane Austen was born.[11]

Hancock's one gift was for securing friends. In India, he became acquainted with Warren Hastings, who stood as Eliza's godfather and was rumored to be Eliza's father. Hastings eventually rose to become the British governor of India, and despite the difficulties of his later years, he amassed a fortune, which he shared freely with Hancock's widow and her daughter.

Philadelphia's brother, George Austen, found assistance closer to home. His uncle Francis, an old-fashioned gentleman who wore a wig and hose and seemed to have stepped out of the previous century,[12] proved a generous and attentive relation. Francis paid for George's education at both the Tonbridge School and later at St. John's Oxford, where George took several degrees. A classicist who enjoyed discussing literature with Warren Hastings,[13] George was ordained to the Anglican ministry in 1754, and was a fellow of St. John's, Oxford, from 1751 until 1760. George's second cousin Jane Monk had married into the wealthy Knight family, who had extensive holdings in Kent and Hampshire.[14] During the eighteenth century, many Anglican churches were more or less the private property of an important family, and the family selected the parish minister and provided his income. The Knights were one such family, and in 1761 they gave George the parish living at Steventon. Not to be outdone, Uncle Francis offered the churches at Deane and Ashe,[15] so that, like a third of the clergy of his time, George Austen was responsible for more than one church parish.[16]

Prior to the eighteenth century, many Church of England clergymen were little more than peasants, with slight education and slighter inclination to elevate culture in the English countryside. Rev. Austen was one of a new breed. With regular features, intense eyes, and a shock of thick hair that earned him the nickname "The Handsome Proctor," George looked like the cultivated, well-read gentleman scholar that he was.[17]

For the new educated clergy of the eighteenth century, a

> clergyman was regarded, both by himself and others, less as a dedicated priest than as an ordinary citizen whose profession it was to represent society in its moral and religious aspects in the same way as a lawyer represented it in its legal aspects. This meant that, if like George Austen, he was conscientious, conducting the Sunday services regularly, christening, marrying and burying his parishioners when required and also keeping a benevolent and paternal eye on their doings in general. These obligations satisfied, his life was much like that of any other respectable country gentleman. He dressed the same, kept the same kind of company, and had plenty of time to occupy himself with whatever interests—scholarly, antiquarian, agricultural—his taste dictated.[18]

The twentieth-century German theologian Karl Barth once remarked that the eighteenth-century clergy throughout Europe was unique in church history: never before had so many such a large number of clergyman devoted so much of their energy to so many activities other than theology. George Austen was no Edward Casaubon, George Eliot's fictional minister who spent more time studying mythology than the Bible, but Austen's range of interests was wide.

Classicist though he was, George was not bound to his studies. Church of England clergymen lived off the combined income of tithes and glebes, the latter a portion of land donated by parishioners for the support of their rector.[19] The glebe land at Steventon was only three acres, so Mr. Knight added the two hundred acres of the Cheesedown farm to the benefice.[20] With the additional acreage, George began pig breeding, and by 1801 had acquired "five cart horses, three sows, twenty-two pigs, three market wagons, four ploughs, eight harrows," as well as other farm equipment.[21] The Austens had enough glebe land not only to fill their own table but also to produce a surplus for sale.

In the midst of his agricultural pursuits, Rev. Austen remained a faithful pastor:

In the course of thirty-seven years as rector of Steventon, he rarely called upon a substitute. All but a handful of births, marriages and deaths were registered by him. He visited parishioners in their homes to baptise their new-born infants before a second Sunday had passed, as the Prayer Book then required. He held services of Morning and Evening Prayer in church every Sunday, and administered the sacrament of Holy Communion often enough for his parishioners to fulfill their obligation to partake of it at least three times a year, one of which had to be Easter. Visitation returns testify that he kept the chancel of his church in good repair, as was his duty, and saw to it that the wardens fulfilled their obligations to maintain the nave, if necessary by levying a rate.[22]

Not every eighteenth-century father could have recognized

Jenny's talents, and fewer still would have encouraged them, but George Austen was the perfect father for a young writer. Possessed of a library of some five hundred volumes, George enjoyed reading and writing and passed on these amusements to his daughters and sons. In the (biased, of course) opinion of his son Henry, he was "a profound scholar, but possessing a most exquisite taste in every species of literature, it is not wonderful that his daughter Jane should, at a very early age, have become sensible to the charms of style."[23] He read romances and poetry to the family, and the one book that still survives with his signature and bookplate is *Reliques of Irish Poetry* by Charlotte Brooke.[24] Her father was often in Jane's mind. When she met a Mr. Wilkes, "an easy, talking, pleasantish young man," who was studying classics at St. Johns, Cambridge, she listened as he "spoke highly of H. Walter as a Schollar;—he said he was considered as the best Classick in the university." Austen immediately thought, "How such a report would have interested my Father!"[25]

Jenny imbibed her father's resolute eighteenth-century moral and religious commitments as well as his literary taste. When her brother Francis left the Royal Naval Academy to go to sea in 1788 (at the age of fourteen), his father wrote lengthy letters instructing him on proper conduct as a man and seaman. It is sturdy eighteenth-century advice, emphasizing propriety, honorable behavior, and, especially, prudence. "Prudence," he wrote, "extends to a variety of objects. There is never any action of your life in which it will not be your interest to consider what she directs! She will teach you the proper disposal of your time and the careful management of your money—two very important trusts for which you are accountable."[26] Rev. Austen taught his children the duty of prayer, morning and night, an absolute "[d]uty which nothing can excuse the omission of." Though he was a man of the *Prayer Book*, he encouraged Francis to recall that "a short Ejaculation to the Almighty, when it comes from the heart will be as acceptable to him as the most elegant and studied form of Words."[27] In his own mind, George Austen's most important contribution to his children's education was to direct them to the highest end of man, that "first & most important of all considerations to a human Being," which is "Religion."[28] Jenny learned this lesson alongside her siblings.

POET OF THE FAMILY

If Jane acquired her father's literary tastes and style, she inherited her energy, her comic spirit, her talent for epigrams, and her sometimes violent wit from her mother, Cassandra (nee Leigh; 1739–1827), whom George Austen married in 1764. Cassandra was better connected than her husband, both socially and academically, and her silhouette displays the haughty aquiline nose that, in her opinion, constituted proof of aristocratic heritage. Long before, her ancestor Thomas Leigh, Lord Mayor of London during Elizabeth's reign, died with enough wealth to endow two sons with lands. One branch of the family settled at Adlestrop in Gloucestershire, while the descendants of a younger son went at Stoneleigh in Warwickshire. The Stoneleigh Leighs advanced to a peerage during the English Civil War by giving refuge to King Charles I when he was denied entry to the city of Coventry, but by the mid-eighteenth century this branch of the family was nearly extinct.[29]

Cassandra Leigh came from the lesser but more long-lasting Adlestrop Leighs, noted more for their intellectual attainments than wealth or social position. James White, the founder of St. John's, Oxford,[30] was in the family tree, and Cassandra's uncle, Theophilus Leigh, was "a personage well known at Oxford in his day, and his day was not a short one, for he lived to be ninety, and held the Mastership of Balliol College for above half a century." Uncle Theophilus was better known for "his sayings than his doings, overflowing with puns and witticisms and sharp retorts. While a fellow of Corpus Christi College, the Fellows of Balliol elected him Master, his main qualification being his frailty and age, which would, they expected, lead to his early demise. As one of Jane Austen's nephews wrote later, Theophilus Leigh's "most serious joke was his practical one of living much longer than had been expected or intended." He lived on as Master of Balliol, and outlasted many of the conniving Balliol Fellows who voted him in. Cassandra's father, Thomas Leigh, nicknamed "Chick" because of his youth when he entered Oxford, was a Fellow at All Souls, Oxford, and held the College Living at Harpsden.[31]

At the age of six, her uncle Theophilus had already dubbed Cassandra the "poet of the family,"[32] and she wrote verse throughout her life, much of it doggerel impressive more for its vigor than its craftsmanship. When one of her husband's students remained on Christmas holiday too long, Cassandra urged him to return:

Of Dan Virgil, we say
Two lessons each day,

And the story is quite entertaining;

You have lost the best part,

But come, take good heart,

Tho' we've read six, there's six books remaining.[33]

Cassandra's relations shared her literary bent. Her first cousin, Mary Leigh, daughter of Theophilus, wrote novels that have been lost, and Mary's younger sister, Cassandra Cooke, published a novel, *Battleridge*, in 1799. But the Cookes' location was more significant than their literary production. The Cooke house in Surrey was opposite the home of the literary sensation Fanny Burney, Madame d'Arblay, author of *Camilla* and *Ceclia*, and the families were intimate enough for Mrs. Cooke to suggest that Burney publish *Camilla* by subscription, an arrangement that made Burney one of the richest writers of her time. Jane Austen was on the list of subscribers, and she must have glimpsed the author during her frequent visits to the Cookes, though there is no evidence she ever met Burney, much less evidence that Jenny wanted to meet her.[34]

Despite her august ancestry, Cassandra was a practical woman and an energetic housekeeper. She devoted her time to cooking, overseeing work in the garden and on the farm, managing the house, sewing clothing for her large family, and maintaining discipline of her own children and later of her husband's students. She loved the countryside around Steventon and disliked urban life. After a visit to London, she observed "'tis a sad place, I would not live in it on any account: one has not time to do one's duty to God or man."[35] She was involved in her husband's farming activities enough to track the weather, the growth of wheat, and the need for dry weather for peas and oats.[36] She was unpretentious: "It didn't bother her that she was forced to arrive for the first time at her new home sitting alone with many of her belongings on a feather bed perched on top of a wagon; the track leading to Steventon Rectory was too rough going for any more genteel conveyance."[37] She went visiting in the neighborhood wearing the scarlet suit she had worn to her wedding.[38] When her daughter-in-law, Elizabeth, went into labor late one April night in 1793, Mrs. Austen, then in her fifties, rose from bed and trudged a mile and a half carrying a lantern to attend the birth.[39] Even late in life, she still worked long hours in the garden.[40]

Mrs. Austen denied that she had ever been good-looking, but her granddaughter Anna Lefroy remembered an attractive woman with gray, peculiarly tinted eyes, an aristocratic nose and thin face, with a thin, spare figure and dark hair.[41] She was proud of her children, but expressed her love in a typically angular way: "I want to show you my Henry and my Cassy," she wrote to Philadelphia Walter, daughter of William Hampson Walter, in 1773, "who are both reckoned fine children," almost immediately adding, "I have got a nice dairy fitted up and am now worth a bull and six cows, and you would laugh to see them for they are not much bigger than Jack-asses." Henrys and Cassys and bulls and cows—they were all one: "you must come, and, like Hezekiah, I will show you all my riches."[42] Jane did not get on altogether well with her mother. Though she outlived her famous daughter by more than a decade, Mrs. Austen was a hypochrondriac, and Jane often found her complaints exasperating. Perhaps they were too alike to mesh smoothly.

Like George, Cassandra had siblings who played an important role in the lives of her children. Her brother, James, benefited from the generosity of his aunt, Miss Anne Perrot. When Miss Perrot's brother died and gave his estate to her, she insisted on passing it on to her nephew James, who adopted the Perrot name. He married Jane Cholmeley, and after living for a time at the ancestral Perrot estate at Norleigh, they sold it and moved to Scarlets and later to the Paragon in the city of Bath. When Jane refers to "my uncle" and "my aunt" in her correspondence, she is referring to her uncle James and aunt Jane Leigh-Perrot.[43]

MUCH SPIRIT AND VIVACITY

The Austens were a lively, spirited, unified family. Jane's niece Caroline remembered:

> In the time of my childhood, it was a cheerful house—my Uncles, one or another, frequently coming for a few days; and they were all pleasant in their own family—I have thought since, after having seen more of other households, *wonderfully*, as the *family* talk had much of spirit and vivacity, and it was never troubled by disagreements as it was not their habit to argue with each other—There was always perfect harmony amongst the brothers and sisters, and over my Grandmother's door might have been inscribed the text, "Behold how good-and how joyful a thing it is, brethren, to dwell together in unity."[44]

Perhaps that's too hazily sepia to be entirely trustworthy, and we find a few cross words in Austen's letters about in-laws. Yet by every indication the Austen family got on well, unified by common interests, tastes, and enthusiasms.

It was a predominantly masculine family. The seventh of eight children, Jenny was born into a house already full of children, most of them boys. Her oldest brother, James, left home when Jane was only four but visited Steventon regularly during Jenny's childhood. Born in 1765, he left for training at his father's alma mater, St. John's in Oxford, in 1779 (at age fourteen!), then accepted a call as a curate and later as a vicar. James also enjoyed hunting, and wrote about his delinquency at Oxford whenever he heard the sound of a hunting horn.[45] He was an aspiring poet in the waning tradition of Thomas Gray and William Cowper, and even after Jane began publishing her books, Mrs. Austen, and perhaps others, thought of James as the writer of the family, who "possessed to the highest degree" the knowledge, taste, and "power of elegant composition" required of a poet.[46]

While at University, James edited a literary magazine, *The Loiterer*, which ran for sixty issues during 1789–90 and for which he wrote many of the articles. *The Loiterer* was modeled on the great eighteenth-century literary magazines of Addison and Steele, and the essays combined social commentary, satire, and moral critique in the tradition of Samuel Johnson. James may have provided his little sister her first opportunity to appear in print. A letter signed by "Sophia Sentiment" in the ninth issue of James's magazine is written in a tone uncannily attuned to that of Jenny's *Juvenalia*. Miss Sentiment complained that the editors "have never yet dedicated one number to the amusement of our sex," and speculated that they might hold the opinion of "the Turks" that women "had no souls." She wanted to see "some nice affecting stories, relating the misfortunes of two lovers, who die suddenly, just as they were going to church. Let the lover be killed in a duel, or lost at sea, or you may make him shoot himself, just as you please; and as for the mistress, she will of course go mad." Whatever happens to them, it is essential that "your hero and heroine must possess a good deal of feeling, and have very pretty names."[47] If this was another Austen than Jenny, it is evidence of a remarkable similarity in style and sensibility.

James married Ann Mathew in 1792, who died two years later. In 1797, James remarried to Mary Lloyd, a longtime friend of the Austens, and had a son and a daughter with her. When his father retired from the rectorship at Steventon, he took that position, serving from 1805 until 1819. During his second marriage, he settled into a melancholic funk, perhaps disappointed that, for all his early promise, he never published a poem in his lifetime.

The Austens' second son, George, is almost never mentioned in family records. He lived apart from the family, suffered from some debilitating disease that was likely epilepsy, and was probably deaf and dumb. Jane learned to speak "with [her] fingers," perhaps to communicate with George. Writing to his half brother's wife, Mrs. Walter, in 1770, Jane's father thanked her for "your kind wish for George's improvement," but added, "God knows only how far it will come to pass, but from the best judgment I can form at present, we must not be too sanguine on this Head." He found a silver lining in George's condition: "be that as it may, we have this comfort, he cannot be a bad or a wicked child."[48]

Like his father, the third son, Edward, depended on the kindness of relatives. Edward was born in 1767 and adopted by the Knight family of Kent in his early teens, becoming heir to a considerable estate and fortune. Though he lacked James's intellectual sparkle, he was a careful, sensible businessman,[49] and his fortune proved essential to the family after Jane's father died in 1805. Edward was a natural leader. When Napoleon threatened England, Edward distinguished himself by leading the East Kent Volunteers in patrolling the Kentish coast.[50]

Two of Jane's other brothers, Francis and Charles, entered the navy and served with distinction. A year and a half older than Jenny, Francis—known to his family as Frank—was a strong character, competent and energetic, a man who got things done. Before he was ten, he had bought a pony and sold it for a profit.[51] He entered the Naval Academy at Portsmouth in 1786, and went on his first voyage at the end of 1788. He fought in the Napoleonic Wars (though he was disappointed to miss Trafalgar), served in the Far East, and rose to become an admiral. His daring exploits were the stuff of adventure novels. In one encounter during the Napoleonic Wars, his ship, the *Peterel*, intercepted three French ships simultaneously off the coast of Marseilles, forcing two aground and capturing the third. In the episode, Francis did not lose a man.[52] Frank eventually became commander in chief of the North America and West Indian station, though this happened decades after his sister's death. He had listened to his father's advice, and was known for his upright moral and religious principles. In a time when most naval officers stood during worship, he was known as "*the* officer who knelt in church."[53] He married Mary Gibson in 1806, and they had eleven children.

Being Jenny's only younger sibling, Charles was her "particular little brother." When he was born in June 1779, Jenny finally had someone to lead around, and she took advantage of it. On a summer evening in 1782—when Jane was not yet six, and Charles only three—she tromped out with Charles as far as New Down, following their father who had gone out in a chaise to pick up Cassandra at Andover after her visit to their cousins, the Coopers.[54] Charles was less strict than Frank; he enjoyed dancing and other pleasures, and cut a figure not unlike the dashing soldiers and brave sailors who populate his sister's novels. He married Fanny Palmer in 1807, while serving with the British navy in Bermuda, and during the 1850s, he became commander in chief of the East India and China station.

Jane followed her brothers' naval careers attentively. She was gratified when a man named Early Harwood praised Charles in "extravagant terms" and said that "he is looked up to by everyone in all America."[55] In honor of her brothers, she proudly wore Mary Austen's Mameluke cap to a ball in Kempshott, a kind of fez that became fashionable after Nelson's victory over Napoleon at Aboukir Bay,[56] and she received a topaz cross on a gold chain from Frank after he won forty pounds for his part in defeating French ships off the coast of Spain.[57]

Famously, Jane Austen wrote her novels always from a woman's point of view. For all we know, she never even attempted to describe an all-male scene; there are no extant scenes in the smoking room or club, no scenes of hunting or war, no rough manly male-only conversations among. Men never appear without women, and with women around they are always on their best behavior. This is a deliberate artistic choice. Austen knew that she was ignorant of the inside world of men, and so she avoided trying to depict it in her fiction. Even so, she got some of it wrong. There's a prissiness to some of her male characters, and her men are far more likely to speak about their romances than most real men.

Yet, Austen knew her brothers, and her brothers were hunters, sailors, soldiers, clergymen, men of the world, as well as literate and witty conversationalists. Little Jenny was fascinated by the male world where she saw her brothers frolicking, and wished that she could go hunting to kill some of the birds they left behind. Despite the femininity so obvious in her books, Austen understood and valued masculinity, and several of her male characters are among the most vivid in English literature. Particularly in her early work, Austen displays a rough sense of humor that surely owed something to the male-dominated house in which she was raised. Her first writings were composed for her family's amusement, which meant, in effect, for the amusement of boys and young men. She got them laughing at drunks and sudden deaths, and wrote bluntly about other people's bad breath and insipid silliness. Throughout her life, she continued to write as much for a male audience as for a female. G. K. Chesterton had it right when he commended Austen for being able to do what neither George Eliot nor Charlotte Brontë could do: "she could coolly and sensibly describe a man."

OH! WHAT A HENRY!

Of all her brothers, Austen was closest to the Austens' fourth son, Henry, whom his father thought the most talented. Henry inherited his father's good looks, shared his family's wit, and early on showed promise of being the most accomplished of the Austen brothers. He never quite lived up to the promise, as his life shifted regularly from one path to another. He attended Oxford, spent time in the Oxfordshire militia, and managed a bank. As a young man, he considered following his father and older brother into the ministry, and after his bank failed he entered the church and ended his life as a clergyman. He was serious enough about pastoral ministry that he brushed up on his Greek in preparation for his examination by the bishop, only to be disappointed when the examining bishop commented on how seldom he consulted the Greek New Testament.[58]

Through the ups and downs of his life, Henry remained winning and amiable, hopeful, adaptable, a little impatient, with a lucky knack for worming his way into high society and being in the right place at the right time. In the early summer of 1814, Napoleon was on the defensive as Russians, Prussians, and Austrians invaded France from the east, and the Duke of Wellington marched across the Pyranees to attack from the south. In June, the emperor of Russia and the king of Prussia visited England for a two-week celebration of the impending allied victory, and a magnificent ball was put on by the White's Club at Burlington House. Somehow, Henry got himself invited to hobnob with the Prince Regent of England, the emperor, and the king.[59] "O What a Henry!" Jane exclaimed when she heard.

Henry was attractive and attracted to women. He made and broke one engagement, and probably many more hearts. Years later, when Jane visited him in London, she noticed that he had several "favorites," which he distinguished geographically. Finally, after one lengthy flirtation and at least one rejected proposal, he married the Austens' cousin, the exotic widowed Comtesse Eliza (Hancock) de Feuillide, ten years Henry's senior. Henry found in Eliza a kindred spirit, a woman with the same flair and ease with fashionable society. Eliza was the daughter of Philadelphia Austen Hancock, George Austen's sister, and she inherited her mother's verve and adventurousness. Nothing captures Eliza's personality quite so well as a toss-off line in a letter to her cousin Phylly Walter: speaking of her interest in two Austen boys—after her husband died, she led on both James and Henry—she said, "One cannot bring her mind to give up dear Liberty, and yet dearer flirtation."[60]

As if a birth in India did not make her eccentric enough, Eliza added a French title. Two years after Tysoe Hancock died, Phila had moved with Eliza to France, hoping that she would be able to live more cheaply on the Continent than in London. In some mysterious way, perhaps by relying on connections with Warren Hastings, the two quickly worked their way into the higher reaches of French society. Soon Eliza was writing to her envious cousin, Phylly Walter, about her visits to Versailles where she delighted in the latest court fashions.[61] In 1781, she become engaged to Jean-Francois Capot de Feuillide, ten years older and reputed to be a Comte. They married in December 1781, when Eliza was nineteen, but each soon found that they had been deceived about the other. The Comte did not really deserve his title, and Eliza was not the heiress the Comte had been led to believe. They made the best of it; the Comte, by Eliza's estimate, was excessively in love with her, and Eliza comfortably fond of him.

Eliza and Jean-Francois produced one child, a sickly boy whom they named Hastings, born in June 1786. Eliza and her mother were back in England when the French Revolution broke out in 1789. With her husband busy renovating his family property in France, Eliza fell back on the hospitality of her Steventon cousins until she moved with her mother to London. By early 1794, her husband had fallen out with the revolutionary government, and he was guillotined on February 22 of that year. Eliza's mother, Philadelphia Austen, had died in February 1792, and Eliza, bereft of parents and husband, looked to the Austens for help. They again provided her a place to live, and eventually a new husband. Henry married Eliza on December 31, 1797, and they lived a socially active, childless life until Eliza died in London in April 1813, with her cousin/sister-in-law Jane at her bedside.

Austen's niece Caroline observed, "Aunt Jane was a very affectionate sister to all her Brothers,"[62] but there was little doubt that Jenny was closest to her only sister, Cassandra. Elder by two and a half years, Cassandra was, by Jane's account, the more sensible and useful of the sisters. According to Caroline, Jane began the "habit of looking up to [Cassandra]" in childhood, and "seemed always to continue." She recalled, "When I was a little girl, [Jane] would frequently say to me, if opportunity offered, that Aunt Cassandra could teach everything much better than *she* could—Aunt Cass *knew* more—Aunt Cass could tell me better whatever I wanted to know—all which, I ever received in respectful silence." She noticed that "the most perfect affection and confidence ever subsisted between them."[63] Especially in her youth, Jenny strove to do whatever Cassandra did. "If Cassandra were going to have her head cut off, Jane would insist on sharing her fate," Mrs. Austen quipped. Though Cassandra seems austere and reserved by comparison with her imaginatively playful younger sister, Jane commended her as "the finest comic writer of the present age." Their niece Anna Lefroy later remembered Jane and Cassandra walking together "in wintry weather through the sloppy lane between Steventon & Dean in pattens, usually worn at that time even by Gentlewomen," wearing bonnets "precisely alike in colour, shape & material" so that Anna had to guess which was which. Rev. Austen took to calling them "the Girls" or, no doubt with complete accuracy, "the Formidables."

A HOUSE OF CHARITY

Austen's first world was in Steventon, Hampshire. More narrowly, her world was the home of an Anglican minister. It was a Christian home, and Jane Austen shared the faith of her parents. Her father was the parish minister in Steventon, two of her brothers followed their father into the ministry, and one of the brothers who pursued a naval career was known for the unusual intensity of his piety. Her father led the family in prayer each morning in the parlor, and they all attended church every week.[64] Jane Austen was a P. K., a Preacher's Kid.

Jenny was baptized soon after her birth, and went through

a full christening ceremony in early April 1776.[65] In his biographical sketch of his sister, Henry described his sister's piety: "Jane Austen's hopes of immortality were built upon the Rock of ages. That she deeply felt, and devoutly acknowledged, the insignificance of all worldly attainments, and the worthlessness of all human services, in the eyes of her heavenly Father. That she had no other hope of mercy, pardon, and peace, but through the merits and suffers of her Redeemer."[66] Jane never used such Evangelical language, preferring the more formal cadences of Prayer-Book Anglicanism, but that doesn't falsify the substance of Henry's characterization.

Austen had few books of her own, but one was William Vickers's *Companion to the Altar*, a book of prayers and meditations in preparation for the Eucharist, in which she read passages like "All the blessings which we now enjoy, and hope hereafter to receive from Almighty God, are purchased for us, and must be obtained, through the merits and intercession of the Holy Jesus, who has instituted the Sacrament of the Lord's Supper, for a continual Remembrance of his Death and Passion, to our great and everlasting comfort . . . But then we must remember, that these blessings are no where promised, but on condition that we ourselves are first duly qualified for them."

The Austens' Christianity was not the excitable Christianity of Bunyan or John Newton, but a cooler, more rational and more ethically focused Christianity, which expressed itself chiefly in acts of charity. First Corinthians 13 was the touchstone of the family's faith.

The Austens were not rich. They enjoyed a few imported foods—tea, sugar, chocolate, spices, citrus fruits, occasional spiced foods from India, but in the main they provided food from their own lands. Cows, ducks, chickens, and turkeys roamed the Austens' yard, while potatoes, vegetables, herbs, and fruit grew in their garden. From their own beehives they drew out honey, and fermented it into mead. Their home was furnished by purchases from local and regional craftsmen. Austen's brother James equipped the parsonage at Deane with mahogany furniture that cost over two hundred pounds (a tidy sum in those days), but Jane's father furnished his house with more economy. He bought beds with mahogany knobs for about a pound each, and cotton for the bed hangings for four pounds. The Austens had several servants, but in the eighteenth century "servants" were not a sign of wealth but a kind of household conveniences: "add a servant, add a convenience—hot water, central heating, a washing machine, and so on."[67]

They did not have a great deal, but what they had, they shared, freely and frequently. After their marriage, George and Cassandra lived for four years in the Deane parsonage, gradually paying for modest improvements in the Steventon parsonage. Though newlyweds, they took in Cassandra's widowed mother, who brought with her the seven-year-old George Hastings, son of Warren Hastings. George Hastings soon died of diphtheria, and Mrs. Austen mourned as if he were her own child.[68] James Leigh-Perrot turned over Jane's mentally handicapped maternal uncle Thomas to the Austens' care.[69] When Philadelphia Hancock died of cancer, the Austens assisted her daughter, Eliza de Feuillide, prompting Eliza to describe Jane's father as "the nearest and best beloved relative of the never to be sufficiently regretted parent I have lost."[70] When

Jane Cooper's father died (Mrs. Austen's brother-in-law), leaving her engaged but orphaned, she turned to the Austens for advice and oversight. George Austen stepped in as surrogate father, advised Jane to wait three months, and then presided at her December 11, 1791, marriage to Captain Thomas Williams, commander of the HMS *Lizard*.[71] When the widow Lloyd died, Mrs. Austen brought Martha Lloyd into her home, even though Rev. Austen had died only a few months before. During Jane's later years, when her niece Anna's romantic entanglements created tension with her father and stepmother, she could always find refuge with the Austen women.[72] When Jane's aunt Leigh-Perrot was bizarrely accused of shoplifting a bit of lace in 1799, she was packed off to prison to await trial. Her confinement was comfortable by the standards of the age, but for a lady of Leigh Perrot's stature, it was a hellish experience. Mr. and Mrs. Austen offered their daughters' services, suggesting that Jane and Cassandra move in to help their aunt during her confinement. Aunt Leigh Perrot refused, but the fact that the Austens offered, no doubt with Jane's and Cassandra's consent, is testimony to the level of sacrifice they were willing to endure for relatives or friends.

As the girls grew up, they took on similar causes. Cassandra "took an interest in the poor of the parish, made garments for them, visited those in trouble and taught some of the village children to read."[73] Anne Lefroy, one of Austen's closest friends, worked creatively to better the lives of the poor of Ashe and surroundings: "After marrying the Reverend Mr Lefroy, she turned her attention to philanthropy, throwing herself into welfare work among the poor children of the neighborhood, teaching them to read and write and make baskets and even—for she was a pioneer in health matters—vaccinating eight hundred of them with her own hands."[74]

Jane's two favorite women in the world demonstrated charity to the people of the parish, and Jane followed suit. She gave Cassandra an account of her "charities to the poor" of Steventon, gifts of fabric and clothing: "I have given a pr of Worsted Stockgs to Mary Hutchins, Dame Kew, Mary Steevens & Dame Staples; a shift to Hannah Staples, & a shawl to Betty Dawkins; amounting in all to a half a guinea.—But I have no reason to suppose that the Battys *would* accept of anything, because I have not made them the offer."[75] When a fever became "all the fashion this week in Lyme," Jane pitched in with nursing help:

Miss Anna Cove was confined for a day or two, & her Mother thinks she was saved only by a timely Emetic (prescribed by Dr Robinson) from a serious illness; and Miss Bonham has been under Mr Carpenter's care for several days, with a sort of nervous fever, and tho' she is now well enough to walk abroad, she is still very tall & does not come to the Rooms.—We all of us, attended them, both on Wednesday evening & *last evening*, I suppose I must say, or Martha will think Mr Peter Debary slighted.[76]

When Henry's wife Eliza was on her deathbed in 1813, Jane went to be with her, and she nursed Henry through a serious illness in 1815. Many years later, Anna would summarize novels to Jane while her aunt was "busily stitching away at a work of charity, in which I fear that I took myself no more useful part."[77] A quarter of Jane's expenditures during her stay in Southampton were pew rents and charities.[78] Austen was hardly a radical or socialist, but she knew the evils of poverty and recognized that the wealthy often exacerbate the conditions of the poor. "Mrs. Deedes is as welcome as May to all our benevolence to her son," she wrote in a letter, "we only lamented that we could not do more and that the 50? we slipped into his hand at parting was necessarily the limit of our gift."[79]

Charity did not come naturally to Jane. She had a childish selfish streak, and was too sharply observant, too amused and appalled and provoked by human folly, to be entirely gentle or sympathetic. But her prayers show that she saw this as a fault, and she prayed for a gentler, kinder heart. She took to heart a comment by Betty Londe, who asked about Cassandra and "seemed to miss you very much, because you used to call upon her very often. This was an oblique reproach at me, which I am sorry to have merited, and from which I will profit."[80]

Rev. George Austen taught Jane and the rest of the family the duty of charity in the same hierarchical eighteenth-century way that he taught her brother Francis: "With your Inferiors," he wrote to his son, "you will have but little intercourse, but when it does occur, there is a sort of kindness they have a claim on you for, & which, you may believe me, will not be thrown away on them."[81] It was a lesson that left a lasting impression on little Jenny, who grew up to write *Emma*, one of the great English novels about charity.

2

EDUCATING JENNY

I think I may boast myself to be, with all possible vanity, the most unlearned and uninformed female who ever dared to be an authoress." So Jane Austen wrote to the Reverend James Stanier Clarke in 1815.

Jane Austen's self-assessment may strike readers as basically right. She had limited formal education and little exposure to the world, and from the absence of the wider world in her novels, one might conclude she not only lived an uneventful and restricted life but possessed a constricted, narrow, and incurious mind. There are no learned allusions to Homer, Athanasius, and Shakespeare as one finds in Joyce, no evidence of deep historical research, no highbrow flourishes, no sign that she could see past the petty parochialisms of her class and location. Despite all that was happening about her—the American and French Revolutions, the Napoleonic Wars, the Romantic movement in poetry and other arts, the evangelical revival in the Church of England—she chose to focus on a few families in the rural backwaters of Southern England. The world she depicted was rapidly being overtaken by a very different world, the urbanized and industrialized England painted so vividly by Charles Dickens during the middle years of the nineteenth century, but readers find few signs that Jane even noticed it was happening. A spinster daughter of a country parson must have been as shriveled intellectually as she was sexually—so many assume.

Glimmers of interest in the wider world shine through here and there, but are just enough to prove the contrary. Sir Thomas in *Mansfield Park* has plantations in Antingua, and there are some passing references to the slave trade, greatly expanded in the 1999 film adaptation. *Persuasion* focuses on officers of the British navy, and *Pride and Prejudice* teems with soldiers, though their main job in that novel is to dance and look delicious enough in their cherry-red coats at balls to set young female hearts aflutter.

But we can tell from the tone of Jenny's letter that she was joking when she wrote to Rev. Clarke, and readers who think her uneducated and incurious do not read very attentively.

It is true that her formal education was very limited. Twice, the Austens decided to send the girls away to school. In 1783, when Cassandra was ten and Jane seven, they went to Oxford to be students of Mrs. Cawley, the widow of a relative of Mrs. Austen's whose husband had been principal of Brasenose College, Oxford. The Austen girls were accompanied by their older cousin Jane Cooper, the daughter of Jane (Leigh) Cooper, Mrs. Austen's sister. Their brother James was already at Oxford, and the proximity of the school meant that he could keep an occasional eye on his younger sisters. Within a few months, Mrs. Cawley unexpectedly and inexplicably moved the school to Southampton, where much of the student body contracted typhus. Jenny nearly died, and Jane Cooper's mother became infected and did die. The Austens brought their daughters home and planned what to do next.

While in Oxford, Jenny observed things that left her eager to indulge her satiric streak. "I never, but once, was in Oxford in my life," one of her early characters says, "and I am sure I never wish to go there again—they dragged me through so many dismal chapels, dusty libraries, and greasy halls, that it gave me the vapours for two days afterwards."[1]

In the spring of 1785, the Austens placed the girls in the Reading Ladies Boarding School, known as the Abbey School because it was built on the ruins of an old monastery near Reading. The school certainly had the look of a place of learning, housed as it was in the monumental arched gate of the Abbey, and Jenny and Cassandra learned sewing, dancing, writing, arithmetic, French, history, and music.[2] The headmistress, Mrs. Sarah La Tournelle, had been born Esther Hackitt, but took on the French name as a marketing ploy. She spoke no French,[3] and it soon became clear that she was not as devoted to educating girls as she was to the theater. Known for her artificial leg made of cork (the origins of which were as mysterious as her French surname), she delegated the teaching to tutors. The girls stayed at the Reading School until the end of 1786, and then came home for good.

Coming home was hardly a blow to the girls' education, since home was more stimulating by far than any school their parents could afford. At the Steventon rectory, Jenny was surrounded by readers as eager as she, not to mention writers and poets. "We love, & much enjoy with ivory knife/ To sever the yet damp & clinging leaves/ Of some new volume," wrote Jenny's oldest brother James. He added, "Authors too ourselves/ Not seldom."[4] It was the perfect home for an aspiring writer.

Besides, the Steventon rectory was already a school. Even with the extra income from the Cheesedown Farm, the Austens were not financially solvent. From 1770 on, George's finances were dwindling, as he gradually sold off all of the 800*l* he had in an Old South Seas Annuity. In 1773, he borrowed several hundred pounds from Cassandra's brother, James Leigh-Perrot. Finally, the Deane living came available, but even that did not solve the financial difficulties.[5] George Austen did what many of his fellow clergy did in similar circumstances: he took in boys and turned his home into a school.

A MIND IMPROVED BY EXTENSIVE READING

Jenny and Cassy didn't get the attention the boys received, but they breathed the literate atmosphere. Mrs. Austen had taught her girls to read, and Jenny learned history from children's history books, and read moralistic tales like *The History of Little Goody Two-Shoes*, then published by John Newbery.[6] From her brother Edward Jenny received Thomas Percival's *A Father's Instructions of his Children, Consisting of Tales, Fables and Reflections: Designed to Promote the Love of Virtue, a Taste for Knowledge, and an Early Acquaintance with the Works of Nature.* Years later, she met Percival's son, a physician, whom she described as "the son of a famous Dr Percival of Manchester, who wrote moral tales for Edward to give me."[7]

She studied French from Fables choisis, and learned Italian.[8] When her aunt Philadelphia Hancock visited from France, she brought the twelve volumes of Arnaud Berquin's L'ami des enfants for her eleven-year-old niece. Jane owned a copy of Elegant Extracts, a compilation of good writing and good morals, and began to read Samuel Johnson early on, her copy of Rassalas evidence of C. S. Lewis's claim that Austen was Johnson's intellectual, moral, and stylistic "daughter."[9] The girls received art lessons from John Claude Nattes, who would later become a famous watercolor painter.[10] Jenny shared a French book with her brother Francis,[11] and she may have studied her father's globe and looked through his microscope when he was not busy with his students.[12] With his help, she explored his sizable library, and she supplemented her reading list by subscribing to reading societies, both in Steventon and later in Chawton.[13]

Jenny learned piano from Mr. Chard, a future organist at Winchester Cathedral,[14] and she continued to play into adulthood. Much later, a "piano forte" was brought to the Chawton Cottage, and she played every day early in the morning, in a back room where she would disturb no one. When they moved to Castle Square, she was excited to discover that the family would have access to a piano: "Yes, yes, we *will* have a Pianoforte, as good a one as can be got for 30 Guineas—& I will practise country dances, that we may have some amusement for our nephews and nieces, when we have the pleasure of their company."[15] During a sickness, her one comfort was that, because of her inability to read or write, she would spend most of her time becoming more proficient at the piano.[16] Caroline remembered that

Aunt Jane began her day with music—for which I conclude she had a natural taste; as she thus kept it up—tho' she had no one to teach; was never induced (as I have heard) to play in company; and none of her family cared much for it. I suppose, that she might not trouble *them*, she chose her practicing time before breakfast—when she could have the room to herself— She practised regularly every morning—She played very pretty tunes, *I* thought—and I liked to stand by her and listen to them; but the music, (for I knew the books well in after years) would now be thought disgracefully easy—Much that she played from was manuscript, copied out by herself—and so neatly and correctly, that it was as easy to read as print.[17]

Anna Lefroy added that Jane thought little of her own skill:

[N]obody could think more humbly of Aunt Jane's music than she did herself; so much so as at one time to resolve on giving it up. The Pianoforte was parted with on the removal from Steventon, and during the whole time of her residence at Bath she had none. In course of time she felt the loss of the amusement, or for some other reason repented of her own decision; for, when settled at Chawton she bought a Pinaoforte and practised upon it diligently—This, as I understood at the time, she found necessary in order to recover that facility of fingering, which no doubt she had once possessed.[18]

Jenny mocked unnecessary displays of learning. She and Cassandra exchanged thoughts on *Coelebs in Search of a Wife*, a novel by the Evangelical activist writer Hannah More. When

Jane initially misspelled the name as "Caleb," Cassandra corrected her, prompting Jane to respond that the name "Caleb" was the only redeeming quality of the book (which she had not read!). She wondered if More's spelling of *Coelebs* was a signal that the book was intended only for classical scholars. Even so, Austen did make literary allusions, in both letters and novels. During a trip to London, she was disappointed to learn that *Hamlet* had been substituted for *King John* at an outing she was going to attend there, and she did not seem thrilled at the prospect of seeing *Macbeth*.[19] She knew Shakespeare well enough to make passing allusions in her letters. She and Cassandra had disagreed about the relative ages of two Plumptre daughters, but Cassandra was right: "Your answer about the Miss Plumptres proves you as fine a Daniel as ever Portia was;—for I maintained Emma to be the eldest."[20] She was alluding to Portia from *The Merchant of Venice*, who is described as a "Daniel" in the climactic trial scene of that play because of her resemblance to the Daniel of Apocryphal stories about Daniel's sleuthing abilities. Classical references occur occasionally. She expected a report on a ball at Basingstoke from what she called "my Myrmidons," the Greek tribe to which Homer's Achilles belonged.[21] Her biblical allusions were usually jokes. A trip in which various people arrived at a ball by different modes of transport reminded her "of the account of St. Paul's Shipwreck, where all are said by different means to reach the Shore in safety."[22] In one of her letters to James Stanier Clarke, she commented on the "sacrifices of Time and Feeling" required of anyone who would be at court. She struck out a line in her letter alluding to Paul's encouragement that ministers be paid for their labors: "In my opinion not more surely should They who preach the Gospel, live by the Gospel, than They who live *in* a Court, live by it."[23]

From her early youth on, Jenny was avid for history. An extant copy of Goldsmith's *History of England* includes her precocious marginal comments. "Always ill-used, *betrayed and neglected*," she wrote of the Stuarts, and "Oh! Oh! the Wretches!" she exclaimed beside a passage describing the Puritans. She disliked Whigs for attempting to prevent the Scots from wearing kilts: "I do not like this; every ancient custom ought to be sacred, unless it is prejudicial to Happiness"[24]—this when Austen was about twelve. Once, as she prepared to visit Mary Lloyd in November 1800, Mary suggested that she bring some books. Jane protested. "I come to you to be talked to, not to read or hear reading," she said, "I can do *that* at home." But she promised to fill her mind with interesting information to "pour out on you as *my* share of Conversation." At the time, she was reading Robert Henry's six-volume *History of Great Britain*, and she promised Mary to "repeat to you in any manner you prefer, either in a loose, desultory, unconnected strain, or dividing my recital as the Historian divides it himself, into seven parts." Henry's history covered "The Civil &—Religion—Constitution—Learning & Learned Men—Arts & Sciences—Commerce Coins & Shipping—Manners." If she read the whole before she arrived at Mary's, then "for every evening of the week there will be a different subject." Though the Friday discussion of Commerce, Coin, and Shipping would be "the least entertaining," the examination of Manners that followed on Saturday "will make amends."[25]

Her uncle James Leigh-Perrot was not blundering when he gave his twenty-something niece a copy of John Bell's

Travels from Saint Petersburg, and his gift of the Renaissance romance *Orlando Furioso* no doubt pleased her equally.[26] When her nephew James Edward was eight, she gave him *The British Navigator, or, A collection of voyages made in different parts of the world*,[27] and it seems likely that Aunt Jane thumbed through it before passing it on to her nephew.

As an adult, Jane was a reader of sermons, though a discriminating one. She enjoyed Henry's sermons,[28] but disliked the best-selling evangelical sermons of her cousin, Rev. Edward Cooper. She was displeased because he was "fuller of Regeneration & Conversion than ever—with the addition of his zeal in the cause of the Bible Society."[29] From Jane's vantage point, Cooper, who had once collaborated with James Austen on the *Loiterer*, was the kind of man who would believe himself "obliged to purge himself from the guilt of writing Nonsense by filling his shoes with whole pease for a week afterwards."[30] She read William Gilpin's works on landscapes and the Picturesque. Typically, she both appreciated Gilpin's observations and found them amusing. In *Northanger Abbey*, she poked fun at his technical terminology and theories, especially his notion of "the horrid."[31]

Among the books in Rev. Austen's library were the poetic works of William Cowper, from which he would sometimes read aloud.[32] In Jenny's estimation, Cowper ranked above all other poets of her time. Born in 1731, Cowper combined intense, occasionally terrifying, religiosity with a deep, conservative appreciation of natural beauty. In collaboration with the evangelical hero John Newton, Cowper wrote a volume of hymns, the *Olney Hymns*. His translation of *The Iliad* and *The Odyssey* into English verse was one of the most significant after

Alexander Pope's translations. Jenny loved syringas "for the sake of Cowper's line,"[33] a reference to a portion of *The Task*, in which Cowper writes of Laburnum, rich/ In streaming gold; syringa, iv'ry pure" (6, 149–50). Lines from Cowper slip into Austen's prose: "I am now alone in the library, Mistress of all I survey,"[34] she wrote during an autumn visit to Godmersham, quoting from Cowper's poem "Verses Supposed to Be Written by Alexander Selkirk," which begins "I am monarch of all I survey." Cowper's most famous work, *The Task*, is in part a lament for the loss of the traditional English countryside. As Cowper saw things, the English lust for "improvement" spoiled both nature and the English character. Austen might have had the poem open as she wrote *Mansfield Park*, which returns again and again to the question of "improvements" in English manners and morals.

Though Austen never mentioned the great Romantics as among her favorite poets, she was familiar with Wordsworth and Byron, and perhaps with others. As one scholar says, "[Sir Walter] Scott and [the poet Lord] Byron . . . are alluded to prominently in *Persuasion*" and in *Sense and Sensibility*, "Scott is mentioned . . . as among the favorite authors of Marianne Dashwood" and in *Mansfield Park* "is quoted admiringly by Fanny Price; and both poets are referred to in the letters, Scott several times, Byron once." Austen put some of these writers to satirical uses, but that is not a sign of dislike: "For Austen, satire was the sincerest form of flattery."[35]

Most of all, Jenny read novels, encouraged by the example of her father, whose tastes inclined as much to romances like *Midnight Bell* by Francis Lathom as to Cowper and the classics.[36] Jenny and Rev. Austen were not alone in their delight in novels. When a subscription library opened nearby, Mrs. Martin, the librarian, tried to encourage participation by telling everyone that "her Collection is not to consist of Novels, but of every kind of Literature." Austen did not think this would be an inducement to her family, "who are great Novel-readers & not ashamed of being so."[37] Jane's first surviving letter makes reference to Henry Fielding's *Tom Jones*, racy enough reading material for the young daughter of a respectable country parson.[38] She read the romances and Gothic novels that were popular in her time—stories from Maria Edgeworth, Fanny Burney, and numerous lesser authors—novels she mercilessly satirized in her *Juvenalia* and *Northanger Abbey*. Like all successful satire, Austen's depended on extensive exposure to the object of satire. The late eighteenth century was awash with novels of sentiment, which depicted the rapturous feelings of the heroes and heroines, and with Gothic novels, picturesque tales of horror set in exotically haunting settings. Austen devoured these novels, but not because she wanted to imitate them. She enjoyed the effects they had, but even more enjoyed the absurdity of the feelings they depicted. Many of her earliest forays into writing were burlesques of these popular genres.

Samuel Richardson's *Sir Charles Grandison* left a deeper impression. Jane is reputed to have read Richardson's cumbersome volume so often that she nearly memorized the thing, delighting in Richardson's fine psychological sense but also roused to satire by the melodramatic characters and situations. As a self-inflated paragon of perfection, Grandison's character was amusing to Austen, and she made one of her juvenile characters, Charles Adams, a pompous parody. Yet, she also recognized Grandison's virtues, and based Darcy's character partly on Richardson's hero.[39]

Though Jane's curiosity led to wide reading throughout her life, she advised that her niece Caroline devote even more energy to reading than she had done:

> She [Jane] said—how well I recollect it! that she *knew* writing stories was a great amusement, and *she* thought a harmless one—tho' many people, she was aware, thought otherwise— but that at *my* age it would be bad for me to be much taken up with my own compositions—Later still—it was after she got to Winchester, she sent me a message to this effect—That if I would take her advice, I should cease writing till I was 16, and that she had herself often wished she had *read* more, and written less, in the corresponding years of her own life.[40]

Jenny also received informal literary education from Anne (Brydges) Lefroy, known in the neighborhood as "Madam Lefroy." When George Austen received the Deane living, his uncle Francis sold the living at nearby Ashe to Benjamin Langois, a wealthy London lawyer descended from Huguenots. He in turn gave the living to his nephew, the Reverend George Lefroy, who moved into the Ashe rectory with his wife, Anne, in May 1783. Madam Lefroy could recite sections of Milton, Pope, Gray, and Shakespeare by heart, and had published in the *Poetical Register*. This beautiful woman with lively eyes and copious conversation captured the interest of the precocious Jenny Austen. The two, separated by twenty-five years in age, became fast friends.[41]

Madam Lefroy also gave Jenny an opportunity to meet another author, Anne Lefroy's brother Samuel Egerton Brydges, an aspiring but ultimately frustrated poet who later, in the 1790s, published several successful novels. Jenny never much cared for Egerton's books, or for Egerton. Both she and her father read his *Arthur Fitz-Albini*, and neither enjoyed it. "My father is disappointed," she wrote to Cassandra, "I am not, for I expected nothing better. Never did any book carry more internal evidence of its author. Every sentiment is completely Egerton's. There is very little story, and what there is told in a strange, unconnected way." Brydges had a reputation for drawing his characters directly from life, so Jane was on the lookout for local references, but found few: "There are many characters introduced, apparently merely to be delineated. We have not been able to recognize any of them hitherto, except Dr and Mrs Hey and Mr Oxendon, who is not very tenderly treated."

For entertainment, Jenny did what her characters would later do. She loved dancing and chatting, and was an amusing addition to a social gathering. Her family being too poor to provide dance and etiquette lessons, Jane relied on etiquette books for guidance, books she mocked during Elizabeth and Darcy's first dance in *Pride and Prejudice*.[42] Nor could her father afford a full line of appropriate dresses and a month-long stay in fashionable Bath to expose his daughters to eligible young men.[43] Jane's passion for dancing had to be satisfied within easy reach of Steventon—at Hurstbourne Park, the home of the Earl of Portsmouth; or at Deane House, owned by John Harwood; or at Hackwood Park, where Lord Bolton's son Charles tried to get Jane to kiss him; or with the Biggs of Manydown, where

Jane and Cassandra were often overnight guests; or at the Vyne, the home of William John Chute, M.P. and Knight of the Shire. Public balls held at the Town Hall at Basingstoke were always enjoyable. Less formal and genteel than the balls held in private homes, the Basingstoke assembly let Jane mingle with the great and the lesser, and enabled her to cut her preparations to a minimum.[44] Her brother Charles learned to dance at the Naval Academy in Southampton, and when on leave in Portsmouth he would escort his sister to a ball.[45]

JUVENALIA

On December 5, 1794, George Austen paid twelve shillings for "a Small Mahogany Writing Desk with a Long Drawer and Glass Ink Stand Compleat," probably as a birthday gift to his daughter, soon to turn nine.[46] He knew how much she would appreciate it. While Jenny was absorbing popular novels and reading history, she was also, sometime in her preteens, beginning to try her hand at writing.

Between the ages of eleven and eighteen, Jenny produced a collection of tales, essays, plays finished and unfinished, for her family's entertainment. Some she composed for performance. During the 1780s, the family put on theatrical productions in the dining room at Steventon, and later turned the barn into a theater. Their plays included the Henry Fielding farce, *Tom Thumb*, which ends with all the characters being killed. Jane shared the family's theatrical flair: "She was considered to read aloud remarkably well," wrote her niece Caroline. "I did not often hear her but once I knew her to take up a volume of

Evalina and read a few pages of Mr Smith and the Brangtons and I thought it was like a play. She had a very good *speaking* voice—That was the opinion of her contemporaries—and though I did not *then* think of it as a perfection, or even hear it observed upon, yet its tones have never been forgotten—I can recall them even now—and I *know* they *were* very pleasant."[47]

She later collected her writings into three "high-quality quarto notebooks" to be passed around the family.[48] Among this collection of twenty-nine works, Jenny included a short epistolary novel, *Love and Freindship*, in which she mocked the popular "novels of sensibility." She made fun of biased historical writers in her *History of England*, which Cassandra illustrated for her, and added a number of plays and other stories. This early work is known as Austen's *Juvenalia*, and it is essential for getting to know Jane Austen, "for in them, and for the first time, we hear her voice."[49] It is, above all, a comic voice:

> Her early works demonstrate that Jane Austen's was primarily and basically a comic genius: her original literary impulse was an impulse to make her reader laugh. . . . Of course, Jane Austen's masterpieces do reveal a profound insight into man's moral nature and, as such, are, in the best sense of the word, extremely serious. But they are none the less comic for that. Man is such an odd animal, such a mixed untidy bundle of follies and inconsistencies and incongruities, that it is impossible for a discerning observer to look at him for long without smiling. Certainly Jane Austen could not; with the result that to the end of her life and in her most penetrating studies of men and women she hardly writes a paragraph unlit by the glint of a smile.[50]

It is a comic voice of a certain timbre. Her imagination was robust and slightly bawdy. She was, to repeat, raised in a house full of boys, and her early stories are full of scandal, drunkenness, death in many gory varieties. Through it all, Austen maintains a tone of lightness and glee: "there is nothing heavy-handed or 'sick' about it, only an impish infectious gaiety."[51] There is an absurdist streak as well, especially in the drama "The Mystery," which includes a scene where a lone character onstage says, "But Hush! I am interrupted" and another in which the characters find that the scene is already over and leave the stage. "The Mystery" prompted Claire Harman to describe teenage Jenny as "a jolly Samuel Becket!"[52] In another age, Austen might have written for *Saturday Night Live*.

A keen reader of histories, Jenny also attempted to write her own. In her *History of England*, written, she said, "by a partial, prejudiced, & ignorant Historian," and illustrated by Cassandra, she described Henry VI's reign:

I cannot say much for this Monarch's Sense. Nor would I if I could, for he was a Lancastrian. I suppose you know all about the Wars between him & the Duke of York who was of the right side; if you do not, you had better read some other History, for I shall not be very diffuse in this, meaning by it only to vent my Spleen against, & shew my Hatred to all those people whose parties or principles do not suit with mine, & not to give information. This King married Margaret of Anjou, a woman whose distresses & Misfortunes were so great as almost to make me who hate her, pity her. It was in this reign that Joan of Arc lived

& made such a row among the English. They should not have burnt her—but they did. There were several Battles between the Yorkists & Lancastrians, in which the former (as they ought) usually conquered. At length they were entirely overcome; The King was murdered—& Edward the 4th ascended the Throne.[53]

Other early works delightedly mock the literary conventions of her day. In *Love and Freindship*, she described the adventures of Laura, Isabel, and Marianne, all of whom possess the quivering passions of the heroines of sensibility. Laura describes herself to Marianne in the third letter:

My Father was a native of Ireland and an inhabitant of Wales; my Mother was the natural Daughter of a Scotch Peer by an Italian Operagirl—I was born in Spain, and received my Education at a Convent in France.

When I had reached my eighteenth Year, I was recalled by my Parents to my paternal roof in Wales. Our mansion was situated in one of the most romantic parts of the Vale of Uske. Tho' my Charms are now considerably softened and somewhat impaired by the Misfortunes I have undergone, I was once beautiful. But lovely as I was, the Graces of my Person were the least of my Perfections. Of every accomplishment accustomary to my sex, I was Mistress. When in the Convent, my progress had always exceeded my instructions, my Acquirements had been wonderfull for my age, and I had shortly surpassed my Masters.

In my Mind, every Virtue that could adorn it was

centered; it was the Rendezvous of every good Quality and
of every noble sentiment.

A sensibility too tremblingly alive to every affliction of
my Freinds, my Acquaintance, and particularly to every
affliction of my own, was my only fault, if a fault it could
be called. Alas! how altered now! Tho' indeed my own
Misfortunes do not make less impression on me than they ever
did, yet now I never feel for those of an other. My accom-
plishments too, begin to fade—I can neither sing so well nor
Dance so gracefully as I once did—and I have entirely forgot
the Minuet Dela Cour.[54]

Much of Jenny's early writing is pure nonsense. One evening Laura is sitting with her parents when there is a knock at
the door:

My Father started—"What noise is that," (said he). "It sounds
like a loud rapping at the door"—(replied my Mother). "It
does indeed," (cried I). "I am of your opinion; (said my
Father) it certainly does appear to proceed from some uncom-
mon violence exerted against our unoffending door." "Yes
(exclaimed I) I cannot help thinking it must be somebody
who knocks for admittance." "That is another point (replied
he); We must not pretend to determine on what motive the
person may knock—tho' that someone does rap at the door, I
am partly convinced."[55]

There are more serious touches as well, though glazed over
with adolescent irony. Already she knew something of human

psychology, which she described with wicked accuracy: "the intimacy between the Families of Fitzroy, Drummond, and Falknor, daily encreased till at length it grew to such a pitch, that they did not scruple to kick one another out of the window on the slightest provocation."

Her stories are full of knockabout farce that hardly fits the later perception of Divine Jane. In "The Beautiful Cassandra," written in twelve incredibly brief chapters, the title character buys a bonnet and then goes out to seek her fortune. Her first adventure is at a baker's, where she "she devoured six ices, refused to pay for them, knocked down the pastry cook, and walked away." She takes a coach to Hampstead, and then orders the driver to turn around and take her back where she came from. In the end, she realizes she has no money to pay for her trip, and when the man "grew peremptory," she solves the problem: "She placed her bonnet on his head and ran away."[56]

In another story, Sir William Mountague falls in love with three sisters at the same time, and, unable to decide among them, leaves the country for a village near Dover. Eventually, he makes his way to Surrey, where he falls in love with Miss Arundel, the beautiful niece of Mr. Brudenell. Unfortunately, she prefers a Mr. Stanhope, so "Sir William shot Mr Stanhope; the lady had then no reason to refuse him; she accepted him, and they were to be married on the 27th of October." When Mr. Stanhope's sister, Emma, shows up on the twenty-fifth demanding recompense for her brother's death, "Sir William bade her name her price. She fixed on 14s. Sir William offered her himself and Fortune. They went to London the next day and were there privately married." Two weeks after his marriage, he falls "violently in love" with another woman he spies entering a carriage on Brook Street, and the story trails off with an ellipsis.[57]

WHIMSICAL AND AFFECTED

Clever, articulate, keen, and precocious children do not always please, and Phylly Walter was not pleased with Jane. When the Austen girls visited Uncle Francis, George Austen's benefactor, at Sevenoaks, Phylly wrote to her brother to complain. Cassandra was passable, but Jane was disagreeable: "The youngest is very like her brother Henry, not at all pretty & very prim, unlike a girl of twelve; but it is hasty judgment which you will scold me for."[58] She found Jane "whimsical and affected." Poor Phylly Walter got her subject half right. There is little to suggest that Jane was affected, but there is much that suggests her whimsical playfulness. Everyone who knew her commented on her highly developed sense of the ridiculous, her playful good humor. Much later, Charlotte Maria Middleton remembered Jane as "a tall thin spare person, with very high cheek bones great colour—sparkling Eyes not large but joyous and intelligent." What most struck her was "her keen sense of humour," which "oozed out very much in Mr. Bennett's style." By contrast, Cassandra seemed "very lady-like but very prim."[59]

Others besides Phylly Walter left their impressions of young Jenny. Mary Russell Mitford, whose mother lived near Steventon, remembered her mother describing a twenty-something Jane as the "prettiest, silliest, most affected, husband-hunting butterfly."[60] On the other hand, Eliza de Feuillide gushed, "I hear her sister and herself are two of the prettiest girls in England . . . perfect beauties and of course gain hearts by dozens."[61] A somewhat less prejudiced observer, Madam Lefroy's brother, described Jane as "fair and handsome, slight and elegant."[62]

Her physical appearance is impossible to recover. Family members describe her as tall, more than "middle height," with a graceful and firm walk, "bright hazel eyes," and "mottled skin." Her niece Caroline remembered her having a "bright, but not a pink colour—a clear brown complexion." They had trouble describing her hair—everything from "darkish brown" to "light brunette," and the remaining lock of hair is too faded to be of help in deciding the case.

Cassandra, the family artist, painted her sister twice during her lifetime. One painting shows Jane sitting in the grass with her back to the painter, even her hair invisible beneath her ubiquitous bonnet. The dowdy figure is awkwardly drawn, so it is impossible to get any sense of her body. Cassandra also painted a miniature portrait, but Jane's face looks so sourly screwed that we can hardly believe it is an accurate portrayal, or at least a flattering one. When Austen's nephew James Edward Austen-Leigh published his memoir in 1870, he used a softened, Victorianized version of the miniature. No other visual evidence exists. We have a portrait of George Austen whose electrifying eyes bore into the viewer, and various arresting depictions of her brothers. We even have a silhouette of Jane's mother, Cassandra Austen, with her prominent aristocratic nose, and a late silhouette of a stately Cassandra. But virtually nothing of Jane.

Jenny lives on, as no doubt she hoped, in her words.

EARLY MASTERPIECES

usband-hunting butterfly" was a nasty exaggeration, but Jane noticed men and often talked about them. She referred to Harry Digweed, oldest of the Steventon Digweed family, as "dear Harry,"[1] and she playfully told Cassandra that a middle-aged bachelor, James Holder, intended to seduce her.[2] At dances, she accepted offers from John Willing Warren, Tom Chute, and other young men, though some she avoided because of their appalling lack of skill.[3] When John Harwood's hopes for securing Elizabeth Bigg collapsed, Jane noticed, with some fear, that he was paying more-than-usual attention to her.[4] At eighteen, Jenny returned from a visit to her brother Edward infatuated with Edward Taylor's "beautiful dark eyes."[5] Several men found her attractive enough to consider her a potential wife.

While Cassandra was spending Christmas away, Jane met Tom Lefroy at a public ball and again at the Harwoods' home at Deane House. A recent graduate of Trinity College, Dublin, Tom was George Lefroy's nephew, son of his older brother, Anthony-Peter Lefroy, and he so impressed Jane that she bequeathed all her other suitors to Mary Lloyd.[6] Tom was not the boxing, drinking, whoring rebel depicted in the 2007 film *Becoming Jane*, nor was he at odds with his uncle, Benjamin Langlois, who said of his nephew that he had "everything in his temper and character that can conciliate affections. A good heart, a good mind, good sense and as little to correct in him as ever I saw in one of his age."[7] Tom later studied law at Lincoln's Inn, after which he practiced in Ireland from 1797 until his death at the ripe age of ninety-three, a full fifty years after Austen died. By 1852, he had risen to the position of chief justice of Ireland; and late in life, he confessed to a boyish crush on the famous novelist Jane Austen, whom he met during a visit to his uncle and aunt at Ashe in 1796.

A year Jane's senior, Tom shared Austen's passions—dancing, flirting, and reading. They discussed *Tom Jones*, and Jane was certainly taken with the young Irishman. In the first of her surviving letters, she confides to Cassandra,

> You scold me so much in the nice long letter which I have this moment received from you, that I am almost afraid to tell you how my Irish friend and I behaved. Imagine to yourself everything most profligate and shocking in the way of dancing and sitting down together. I *can* expose myself, only *once more*, because he leaves the country soon after next Friday, on which day we *are* to have a dance at Ashe after all. He is a very gentlemanlike, good-looking, pleasant young man, I assure you. But as to our having ever met, except at the last three balls, I cannot say much; for he is so excessively

laughed at about me at Ashe, that he is ashamed of coming to Steventon.[8]

Austen is here in all her ironic splendor. She writes of shocking behavior, but deflates her boast by saying that it amounts to nothing more than dancing and sitting together. She finds him attractive, but withdraws her judgment by admitting that she barely knows him. Much is played for laughs; in part, the mockery is likely self-protection to keep herself from falling for him.

Later the same day, she continued the letter, detailing a visit from Tom and his cousin George to the Steventon rectory. George, Jenny said, "is really well-behaved now," but she added, "as for the other [Tom], he has but *one* fault, which time will, I trust, entirely remove—it is that his morning coat is a great deal too light. He is a very great admirer of *Tom Jones*, and therefore wears the same coloured clothes, I imagine, which *he* did when he was wounded."[9] In Fielding's novel, the "wounding" is the wound of love, and Austen was casting Tom in the conventional romantic role of a heartsick suitor. Whether she actually believed him to be such is difficult to determine. The following week, she wrote to Cassandra to predict, "I rather expect to receive an offer from my friend in the course of the evening. I shall refuse him, however, unless he promises to give away his white Coat."[10] What kind of offer she expected is unclear. While the tenor suggests an offer of marriage, Jane could hardly expect Tom to propose after a week's acquaintance. Austen again undermined her professed hope with another joking reference to his clothing.

It was not to be. The following day, Austen added an appendix to her letter telling Cassandra of Tom's departure: "At length the Day is come on which I am to flirt my last with Tom Lefroy, & when you receive this it will be over." She immediately turns the moment into satire: "My tears flow as I write, at the melancholy idea."[11]

Some in Tom's family blamed him for leading Jane on, and Janeites sometimes blame Madam Lefroy for breaking up what she considered a disadvantageous match. More commonly, responsibility for ending the flirtation is placed on the shoulders of Tom's great-uncle, the supposedly crotchety Benjamin Langlois, who hoped Tom would do what his father, Anthony, had failed to do—marry well to raise the family fortunes. Whatever happened, it did not cause a breach in friendship between Austens and Lefroys. Jane remained on friendly terms with Madam Lefroy, Tom's aunt, and she stayed at Langlois's London home en route to Godmersham, brother Edward's Kent estate, the following year. Soon after Tom returned to Ireland, he married an Irish girl of little immediate prospects (though she later inherited a fortune because of her brother's early death).[12]

When Tom visited his uncle and aunt again, he did not visit the Austens at Steventon, but Jane retained an interest in him for some time. Nearly two years later, Jane visited the Lefroys with her father and was still interested in Tom's activities, though "too proud to make any enquiries." Perhaps discerning her interest, her father filled the gap: "on my father's afterwards asking where he was, I learnt that he was gone back to London in his way to Ireland, where he is called to the Bar and means to practice."[13] George Austen's thoughtful sensitivity to his daughter is never more fully displayed than here.[14]

Jenny was taken more by Tom Lefroy than by the Reverend Samuel Blackall, who Madam Lefroy brought forward as a possible suitor. Jane found him noisy and pompous, and was not disappointed when he failed to appear in Hampshire over the Christmas holidays of 1798: "our indifference will soon be mutual," she wrote Cassandra with relief, "unless his regard, which appeared to spring from knowing nothing of me at first, is best supported by never seeing me."[15]

BY A YOUNG LADY

Jenny's early twenties were marked by losses more tragic than the loss of Tom Lefroy. In 1795, Cassandra had become engaged to the Reverend Thomas Fowle, a former pupil of Mr. Austen's. Tom was not financially prepared for marriage, and the engagement was kept secret while Tom was sent to the West Indies to serve as a chaplain on an expedition sponsored by Lord Craven. In February 1797, the Austens received news from San Domingo that Tom had contracted yellow fever and died. Cassandra never seriously contemplated marriage again, and entered almost immediately into a premature spinsterhood.

While Tom Fowle was heading to the West Indies, James's first wife, Anne, died suddenly and inexplicably in May 1795. James's two-year-old daughter Anna wandered the house calling for her mother, prompting James to send her off to her aunts for feminine attention. James remarried less than two years later, choosing an old family friend, Mary Lloyd, as his second wife. With her sister Martha, Mary had been a friend to Jane and Cassandra, but once she entered the family things fell off. Mary was inconsiderate toward her stepdaughter Anna, who described her as clever, cheerful, amiable, and a good manager, but complained of her abrupt and sharp manner.[16] Mary could not forget that James had once had another wife nor James's one-time flirtation with Eliza de Feuillide, and she was self-conscious about the scars left on her face by smallpox.[17] Jane thought she domineered over her husband, and the effect on the sensitive literary James was frustrating:

> I am sorry and angry that [James's] visits should give more pleasure. The company of so good and so clever a man ought to be gratifying in itself;—but his chat seems all forced, his opinion on many points too much copied from his wife and his time here is spent I think in walking about the house and banging doors or ringing the bell for a glass of water.[18]

Throughout these events, Jane found sufficient leisure to continue writing. Her brothers were steadily leaving home, and with a dwindling household, her father cut back on teaching duties beginning in the early 1790s. By 1796, all the students were gone. Jane and Cassandra continued to share a bedroom, but they fitted up an adjoining room as a private parlor that they liked to call their "dressing-room." Floored with a chocolate-colored carpet, and furnished with a piano and a table with two oval boxes containing materials for sewing,[19] it was a place to retreat and write. Jane Austen had found a room of her own.[20]

During the late 1790s, her output far surpassed her already

impressive body of juvenile work. She wrote *Lady Susan*, an epistolary novella about a beautiful, conniving widow who manipulates all the dolts—male and female—to achieve her will. The book is closer to *Les liasons dangereuses* than to anything Austen wrote later; it is highly accomplished, and Lady Susan is a masterful villainess. During 1795—that is, before she was twenty—Jenny wrote the first version of *Elinor and Marianne*, an epistolary novel that was later rewritten into *Sense and Sensibility*. From October 1796 to August 1797, she wrote *First Impressions*, which later became *Pride and Prejudice*. *Susan*—published posthumously as *Northanger Abbey*—was likely begun in the summer of 1798, and she finished it by early the following summer.

Pride and Prejudice has proven the most enduring and popular of the three early works. It focuses on the romance of the haughty aristocratic Mr. Fitzwilliam Darcy and the witty, strong-willed, but lower-class Elizabeth Bennet. Elizabeth forms an early prejudice against Mr. Darcy because of reports she receives from a handsome young soldier, Mr. Wickham, who grew up on the Darcy estate. Meanwhile, Darcy is falling in love with the sparkling young Elizabeth, whose "beautiful eyes" he grows to admire. Elizabeth severely rebuffs his first, awkward proposal, but when Darcy gives his side of the story of Wickham, she begins to revise her estimate of the man. When Darcy intervenes to save the Bennet family from a scandal involving Elizabeth's younger sister, Lydia, Elizabeth comes to admire him deeply. Despite the objections of Mr. Darcy's overbearing aunt, Lady Catherine de Bourg, Elizabeth and Darcy marry.

Austen's original title for *Sense and Sensibility* names the two principal characters, Elinor and Marianne Dashwood. When their father dies and they receive little assistance from their half brother, John, they are left to eke out a life with their mother in a cottage provided by the generous John Middleton. Marianne is a young woman of high romantic feeling, and she falls wildly in love with the dashing John Willoughby when he rescues her after a fall. When Willoughby suddenly leaves Marianne to pursue a socially advantageous marriage, she is crushed, and only gradually recovers her liveliness. Sobered by her loss, she falls into a quiet love with the older Colonel Brandon. Elinor, meanwhile, is attracted to the diffident Edward Farrers, who is training for the ministry. Standing in the way of her romance is Lucy Steel, a manipulative young woman who is already secretly engaged to Edward. In the end, of course, Elinor, too, gets her man.

Northanger Abbey is a very different sort of book, a parody of the gothic romances of and novels of sensibility that were so popular in Austen's day. These novels were set in old and frightening castles, followed macabre plots, and were populated by characters whose every emotion was openly expressed. Catherine Morland, Austen's female protagonist, has been reading too many of these novels when she visits the spooky Northanger Abbey near Bath, the estate of the Tilney family. She frightens herself into believing that Henry's father is a monstrous murderer, but Henry slowly weans her away from her fantasies and they are, of course, eventually married. The story stands well enough on its own, but Austen's real purpose was to poke fun at other novelists.

By the middle of 1799, Austen had completed three novels, all of which are classics in their way—*Pride and Prejudice* and *Sense and Sensibility* now canonical romances and comedies of manners, and *Northanger Abbey* that rare satire that continues to entertain when the object of its satire is long out of fashion. She was twenty-four.

George Austen knew his daughter had extraordinary talent, and in November 1797 sent a letter to the London publisher Cadell offering a novel by "a young lady," the novel that would later become *Pride and Prejudice*. As was common at the time, he suggested publication by "commission," in which the author assumes the financial risks of publication:

> I have in my possession a novel . . . , comprised in three Vols about the length of Miss Burney's *Evelina*. As I am well aware of what consequence it is that a work of this sort should make its appearance under a respectable name . . . . where you chuse to be concerned . . . what will be the expense of publishing at the Author's risk & what you will advance for the Property of it.[21]

Cadell wasn't interested. They returned the letter without comment.

The next evidence we have of Austen seeking publication comes from 1803, when Henry's attorney, William Seymour, was able to sell an early version of *Northanger Abbey*, then known as *Susan*, for ten pounds to the London publisher Benjamin Crosby & Sons.[22] Austen believed that Crosby promised to publish the manuscript soon, and the book was advertised in Crosby's magazine. Six years later, Jane contacted Crosby to inquire after the manuscript, suggesting with mock deference that it might have been somehow misplaced. Crosby claimed they had no obligation to publish, and offered to sell the manuscript back for ten pounds. Austen had no money at the time, but she later recovered the manuscript and it was published after her death with a biographical preface by her brother Henry.[23] Her books remained unpublished, and she was left to putter with and polish her characters and plots and to offer her books for the amusement of her family.

WHAT STRANGE CREATURES

From what we know of the final products, Jenny arrived early at her characteristic views on marriage, romance, love, women, and morality. They were views taught by her father, shared by her siblings, confirmed by her critical reading of romance novels. Predictable as the shape of Austen's novels are, they often contain important surprises. Darcy's involvement in reducing the scandal of Lydia's elopement with Wickham is unexpected; Edward Farrers's secret relationship with Miss Steele is likely as shocking to us as it is to Eleanor Dashwood. Austen had a "puzzle-solving mind," and she constructed romantic puzzles and hoped for readers who would play along.[24] Yet her first novels are most valuable not because of the inventiveness of their plots or even the fullness of their characterizations, but because of the complex romantic morality that drives the stories. Austen was not an enemy of passion, but she was an enemy of marriages founded entirely on passion. Austen was not an enemy of wealth, but she was an enemy of marriages contracted for advantage. The best marriages in Austen's novels are marriages of minds and temperament, marriages that make both husband and wife more fully themselves. Compare Austen to the latest chick flick, and the difference is apparent in an instant.

Austen remained consistent with her romantic ethics throughout her life, and as her nieces and nephews grew she had opportunities to apply her theories to real-life situations. When her niece Fanny was being courted by John Plumptre, Aunt Jane wrote two letters in response to news that Fanny was thinking about abandoning her engagement. When she first heard that Fanny was breaking off the relationship, she was surprised, "as I had no suspicion of any change in your feelings"; and in fact after she saw Fanny and John together in London, she wrote, "I thought you really very much in love." But given the change, she concluded that this could not be the case: "you cannot be in love," and "you certainly are not at all" in love. She remarked on the oddity of human desires and affects—"What strange creatures we are!"—and she suggested that Fanny's interest in John began to decline as soon as she was sure that he was bound to her: "It seems as if your being secure of him (as you say yourself) has made you Indifferent." Looking back, she realized that John's behavior brought "a little disgust" but only because Fanny was motivated more by "Acuteness, Penetration & Taste, than Love."

Aunt Jane thought John a rare find: "his uncommonly amiable mind, strict principles, just notions, good habits—*all* that *you* know so well to value, *all* that really is of the first importance—everything of this nature pleads his cause most strongly." As she wrote, her defense of John became stronger:

"the more I write about him, the warmer my feelings become, the more strongly I feel the sterling worth of such a young Man and the desireableness of your growing in love with him again." Fanny worried that John's inclination toward Evangelical commitments would be an impediment to love, but Austen assured Fanny she had nothing to fear: "don't be frightened by the idea of his acting more strictly up to the precepts of the New Testament than others." The only defect in his "fine Character" was "Modesty," hardly a fault. If he lacked the sparkling wit of some other men, Jane insisted, that was not a mortal flaw: "Wisdom is better than Wit, & in the long run will certainly have the laugh on her side."[25]

Her second letter pushed in almost the opposite direction, but Austen insisted that she was not abandoning her earlier advice. Though Austen had forcefully defended John Plumtre's character and prospects, she wrote that Fanny "must not let anything depend on [Jane's] opinion. Your own feelings & none but your own, should determine such an important point." She refused to say, "determine to accept him" because "the risk is too great for you, unless your own Sentiments prompt it." Given Fanny's feelings, Austen could not recommend that Fanny renew her relationship: "I cannot wish you with your present very cool feelings to devote yourself in honor to him. It is very true that you never may attach another Man, his equal altogether, but if that other Man has the power of attaching you more, he will be in your eyes the most perfect." "Nothing," she added, "can be compared to the misery of being bound without Love, bound to one, & preferring another. That is a punishment which you do not deserve."[26]

Marriage is challenging enough without the dangers of uncertain affections. Marriage would become intolerable if a husband or wife were bound but had their affections directed chiefly elsewhere. Being bound without mutual affection appeared to Austen a kind of slavery, and she urged Fanny to make a decision, and not permit anyone, including her beloved aunt, to push her into a marriage she would later regret. For Austen, love was something very particular. It is a matter of mutual attachment, not simply a matter of determining the qualities of each person and adding them like a sum.

In the end, Fanny decided against poor Mr. Plumtre, and she did not marry Edward Knatchbull until three years after her aunt's death.

BECAUSE SHE IS A WOMAN

Along with her views on romance, love, and marriage, Jenny was developing her ideas about women. The first stirrings of feminist protest were rumbling in Austen's lifetime. Mary Shelley's mother, Mary Wollstonecraft (1759–1797), wrote the *Vindication of the Rights of Women* in 1792, showing that the rationalist egalitarianism of the French Enlightenment had made inroads into English social and intellectual life. After Austen's death, things tilted in a different direction, as Victorian stereotypes about wiltingly domestic women took hold.

Though Austen's novels follow a conventionally romantic story line, she has often been viewed as an advocate for women. But she is too subtle to fit easily into a spectrum whose poles are "feminist" and "anti-feminist." On the one hand, she created immensely capable and appealing women. Elizabeth Bennet can match wits with anyone, and even when pressured by the imperious and the great, Elizabeth holds fast to her own views and hopes. Though less pugnacious, Emma Woodhouse is more independent, possessing, as Austen tells us in the first line of the novel, everything that a young woman needs for happiness—she is the mistress of a great house, can use her time and energy as she pleases, and answers to no one. Even the women characters who do not sparkle like Elizabeth Bennet can be decisive, and only Fanny Price is truly helpless. Score one for the feminists. On the other hand, Austen's novels are all romances that end with a strong, independent woman seeking and finding the man of her dreams. Elizabeth eventually puts her wit and vivacity into service as Mrs. Fitzwilliam Darcy, and Emma Woodhouse gives up a considerable share of her independence to become Mrs. George Knightley, and super-competent Anne Elliot is able to renew her romance with Captain Wentworth. Score one for the anti-feminists.

In letters, Austen sometimes takes up women's causes. She sided with the Princess of Wales against her libertine husband. When in February 1813 the princess published an open letter to her husband in the *Morning Chronicle*, stating her grievances against him, Austen complained about everyone "sitting in Judgment upon the Princess of Wales's letter." She was more sympathetic to the princess, mainly because of her sex: "Poor Woman, I shall support her as long as I can, because she *is* a Woman, & because I hate her husband."[27] Austen knew princesses of her day could be prisoners, but she felt more keenly the multiply ways that poverty oppresses women. The Price home in Portsmouth was almost unbearable for Fanny and her mother. When she came back home from Mansfield, Fanny Price was ignored and lost within the constant din of domestic life. She felt liberated when Frank Churchill showed up to take her into the open air.

Jane recognized that her singleness gave her freedom that she would have found difficult to give up. She was sympathetic to women who were constantly tied to childbearing and rearing, and realist enough to know that marriage binds a woman to the drudgery of household management. She was also realist enough to know that independent singleness frequently meant poverty. In a remarkable late letter to her niece Fanny, she wrote,

> Single Women have a dreadful propensity for being poor—which is one very strong argument in favour of Matrimony, but I need not dwell on such arguments with *you*, pretty Dear, you do not want inclination.—Well, I shall say, as I have often said before, Do not be in a hurry; depend upon it, the right Man will come at last; you will in the course of the next two or three years, meet with somebody more generally unexceptionable than anyone you have yet known, who will love you as warmly as ever *he* did, & who will so completely attach you, that you will feel you never really loved before.—And then, by not beginning the business of Mothering quite so early in life, you will be young in Constitution, spirits, figure & countenance, while Mrs Wm Hammon is growing old by confinements & nursing.[28]

She predicted that marriage would change Fanny's disposition, and not for the better:

> Oh! What a loss it will be, when you are married. You are too agreable in your single state, too agreable as a Niece. I should hate you when your delicious play of Mind is all settled down into conjugal & maternal affections . . . . I only do not like you shd marry anybody. And yet I do wish you to marry very much, because I know you will never be happy till you are; but the loss of a Fanny Knight will be never made up to me; My 'affec: Niece F. C. Wildman' will be but a poor Substitute.[29]

Her most mature meditation on femininity comes in her final complete novel, *Persuasion*, where the opposition between male and female characters is sharper and more stereotyped than in other novels. In *Persuasion*, Anne Elliot renews her earlier romance with Captain Wentworth, with whom she had been engaged years before. At the time of the engagement, Wentworth was not wealthy enough for the aristocratic Anne, but when he returns from the Napoleonic Wars he is a successful and wealthy man. As we expect, the love between Anne and Wentworth is renewed and they marry. As a character, Anne Elliot represents a departure for Austen. Elizabeth Bennet is almost more masculine than the diffident Darcy, and Edward Farrers, Henry Tilney, and Edmund Bertram are retiring to a fault. Not Captain Wentworth, the manliest man Austen ever created. Anne Elliot, by the same token, is the most stereotypically female heroine Austen ever created; for all her competence when duty calls, she is dependent, somewhat weak, condemned to a more or less useless life.

What makes *Persuasion*'s treatment of these issues intriguing is the fact that Austen sets the whole novel in a specific historical situation. She recognized that sexual stereotypes were hardening in the aftermath of the Napoleonic Wars, also a period of urbanization and industrialization. As the English moved into towns, women's labor was no longer needed as it once was. Meanwhile, the war had produced a battle-hardened natural aristocracy among soldiers and sailors. As women became more dependent, pointless, and helpless, the old aristocracy was being feminized. Vain Sir Thomas Elliot surrounds himself with mirrors and judges a man's worth by the smoothness of his skin. Austen saw the Victorian division of the sexes taking shape after the Napoleonic Wars, and she recognized that the war had a great deal to do with it. Though she finally puts Anne together with her hero, her novel questions whether the emerging dichotomy between sexes is healthy.[30] Had Austen's explorations been taken more seriously at the time, perhaps the feminist over-reaction to Victorianism would never have been necessary.

JOHNSON'S DAUGHTER

Austen's insight into romantic quandaries of her characters, and her relatives, emerges from her moral outlook, which was in large measure the standard Christian outlook of eighteenth-century Anglicanism. Austen believed there was a moral dimension to social behavior. Manners and morals do not exist in separate realms of life. Manners are a moral concern, and morals take specific shape in the gestures of manners. Accordingly, Jane was annoyed that Eleanor Foote, the first wife of Sir Brook B., would encourage her husband to pursue another woman if she died: "A Widower with 3 children has no right to look higher than his daughter's Governness."[31] When Elizabeth Knight died, Jane consulted with Cassandra about the correct mourning costume.[32] Showing proper respect for the dead was not only a social obligation but a moral duty. She was exasperated by the actions of James's second wife, Mary Lloyd: "How can Mrs. J. Austen be so provokingly ill-judging?" she asked after one altercation. "I should have expected better from her professed if not her real regard for my Mother."[33] She worried that the snub would affect her mother: "Now my Mother will be unwell again." The "Mrs. J. Austen" is revealing—not only does it describe her sister-in-law, whom she knew as a friend, with cold formality, but it also emphasizes Mary's obligations to the Austen family.[34] Ground-level behavior, Austen believed, revealed the depths of one's moral character.

Her moral stance was sometimes too rigid to be entirely charitable. Her reaction to the remarriage of the widowed Lady Sondes was typical. The match "surprises, but does not offend me;—had her first marriage been of affection, or had there been a grown-up single daughter, I should not have forgiven her—but I consider everybody as having a right to marry once in their Lives for Love, if they can—& provided she will now leave off having bad head-aches & being pathetic, I can allow her, I can wish her to be happy."[35] Though the remarriage seemed legitimate, Lady Sondes committed a breach of decorum following her marriage: "Lady Sondes is an impudent woman," Austen opined, "to come back into her old Neighbourhood again; I suppose she pretends never to have married before—& wonders how her Father & Mother came to have christen'd her Lady Sondes."[36] She was severe with the rapid marriage of widowed Mrs. John Lyford, who "is so much pleased with the state of widowhood as to be going to put in for being a widow again; she is to marry a Mr Fendall, a banker in Gloucester, a man of very good fortune, but considerably older than herself & with three little children."[37]

This idea of manners and morals carries over into her fiction as well, and in her books her moral outlook merges with an aesthetic attitude. Appreciation of art, music, and literature is a standard of evaluation for Austen's characters. As Gilbert Ryle recognized, "Jane Austen's ethical vocabulary is laced with aesthetic terms, and, save for Catherine, and, interestingly, the Crawfords, moral sense and aesthetic taste are strong or weak together."[38]

Approved characters are characters of educated, though not rarefied, tastes. Darcy is money, and lives in a magnificent stately home, but what strikes Elizabeth is not the richness of his house but the modesty and tastefulness of its design and decor. The Austen characters who most offend and amuse are those interested in ostentatious displays of wealth and privilege. Lady Catherine de Bourg's tastes are gauche and overwrought, and Sir Thomas Elliot's home and lifestyle are full of gaudy kitsch.

Ryle identified Austen as an Aristotelian, but claimed that she firmly separated her moral life from religion. C. S. Lewis was, I think, more accurate in tracing her morality and her comedy to religious sources.[39] The central importance of Austen's piety has, however, been underemphasized by most biographers and critics. In part this is because her piety is so drastically understated; it is a reticent eighteenth-century Anglican piety that barely breathes its own name. She refrains from religious passion, and speaks of Christian truths in a balanced, matter-of-fact manner that lacks existential power and is completely free of the spiritual terrors of a Luther or Bunyan. This can appear to be indifference or rationalism, but it is simply eighteenth-century Christianity. One early reader got her right, commending Austen as a "Christian writer" whose merit is "enhanced . . . by her religion being not at all obtrusive." Religion is "rather alluded to, and that incidentally, than studiously brought forward and dwelt upon. . . . she is more sparing of it than would be thought desirable by some persons; perhaps even by herself, had she consulted merely her own sentiments." Yet, "she probably introduced it as far as she thought would be generally profitable; for when the purpose of inculcating a religious principle is made too palpably prominent, many readers, if they do not throw aside the book with disgust, are apt to fortify themselves with that respectful kind of apathy with which they undergo a regular sermon, and prepare themselves as they do to swallow a dose of medicine, endeavouring to get it down in large gulps, without tasting it more than is necessary."[40] The Reverend G. D. Boyle cited a friend's assessment of Austen's religion:

> Miss Austen, she used to say, had on all the subjects of enduring religious feeling the deepest and strongest convictions,

but a contact with loud and noisy exponents of the then popular religious phase made her reticent almost to a fault. She had to suffer something in the way of reproach from those who believed she might have used her genius to greater effect; but her old friends used to say, "I think I see her now defending what she thought was the real province of a delineator of life and manners, and declaring her belief that example and not 'direct preaching' was all that a novelist could afford properly to exhibit."[41]

Perhaps Jenny had half-listened to too many mediocre, uninspiring sermons to think that sermonizing would be effective in a novel.

Despite her comparative reticence and her careful avoidance of moralizing, Austen's faith was sincere and deep. Church was a normal part of the Austens' weekly routine. "On Sunday we went to Church twice," she wrote to Cassandra.[42] On a wet Sunday in 1807, her brother Frank was the only one who could attend service, but Jane implied that everyone would have gone if weather had permitted. One preacher, Mr. Sherer, was improving: "I heard him for the first time last Sunday, & he gave us an excellent Sermon." He was "a little too eager sometimes in his delivery," but Austen sees that as "a better extreme than the want of animation"[43] Commenting on a scandalous elopement by one Mrs. Powlett, Austen recalled, "She staid the Sacrament I remember, the last time you and I did."[44]

Jane was godmother to the eldest grandchild of John and Elizabeth Littleworth, a farming family in nearby Cheesedown. Mrs. Littleworth was probably Jane's wet nurse and foster mother when she was an infant.[45] According to the 1662 *Catechism of the Book of Common Prayer* that Austen knew, godparents were responsible for three things: "First, that I should renounce the devil and all his works, the pomps and vanity of this wicked world, and all the sinful lusts of the flesh. Secondly, that I should believe all the Articles of the Christian Faith. And thirdly, that I should keep God's holy will and commandments, and walk in the same all the days of my life."[46] By standing as godmother, Austen also promised to urge the child to attend church; teach the Apostles' Creed, the Lord's Prayer, and the Ten Commandments; and encourage "all other things which a Christian ought to know for his soul's health."[47]

Austen also composed prayers, three of which are extant. One includes these petitions:

Look with Mercy on the Sins we have this day committed, and in Mercy make us feel them deeply, that our Repentance may be sincere, & our resolutions stedfast of endeavouring against the commission of such in future. Teach us to understand the sinfulness of our own Hearts, and bring to our knowledge every fault of Temper and every evil Habit in which we have indulged to the discomfort of our fellow-creatures, and the danger of our own Souls. May we now, and on each return of night, consider how the past day has been spent by us, what have been our prevailing Thoughts, Words, and Actions during it, and how far we can acquit ourselves of Evil. Have we thought irreverently of Thee, have we disobeyed thy commandments, have we neglected any known duty, or willingly given pain to any human being? Incline us to ask our Hearts these questions Oh! God, and save us from deceiving ourselves by Pride or Vanity.

Give us a thankful sense of the Blessings in which we live, of the many comforts of our lot; that we may not deserve to lose them by Discontent or Indifference.[48]

The woman who wrote this had the rhythms of the Anglican prayer book in her blood, a deep sense of her own sinfulness, and a desire to live with more humility and gratitude.

Biographers minimize Austen's Christianity mainly because they cannot believe that her acerbic, sometimes childishly cruel wit, her satires of the clerical imbecilities of Mr. Collins and Mr. Elton, her playful silliness, are compatible with deep Christian faith. The prim formal Miss Austen may have been a parson's daughter, but critics cannot believe *Jenny* was a Christian. This is partly an optical illusion. Austen's ninnies are more vivid and memorable than the faithful, but of the dozen clergymen in her novels, only three (Dr. Grant, Mr. Collins, and Mr. Elton) come in for any sort of criticism, and even they are described as being diligent in their clerical responsibilities.

More fundamentally, the assumption that Christian faith is incompatible with a satirical spirit is entirely wrongheaded. Nietzsche's lie that Christianity is a killjoy religion is a demonstrable falsehood. English satire was, after all, the creation of clerics. Austen was hardly the first Christian writer to look skeptically at the clergy. Chaucer did before her, and so did a host of late medieval writers, including William Langland, whose commitment to Christianity no one seriously questions. Reformation satirists mocked the fat friars. Jonathan Swift—the

Reverend Jonathan Swift—combined wit and religion, as did Laurence Sterne—also a reverend. Samuel Johnson was not a cleric, but he was a serious Christian and yet one of the most sharp-witted men of his time. And who can deny the combination of boisterous cheery and profound faith in Lewis and Chesterton? They were Austen's children as she was Johnson's. Not every wit has been a Voltaire.

4

DISRUPTIONS

Like Elizabeth Bennet, Jane Austen was a great walker who enjoyed trekking through towns and cities as well as the countryside. Her letters are full of observations about changing weather, and the effect of thunder and snow not only upon travel but upon her moods. After a pleasant day at nearby Alton, she wrote, "We had a beautiful walk home by Moonlight."[1] Conventional as this may be, it expresses Jenny's genuine delight in the simple fact of a shining moon. When Cassandra was away, Jane kept her abreast of the condition of the vegetable and flower gardens at Chawton Cottage: "Some of the Flower seeds are coming up very well—but your Mignioette makes a wretched appearance. . . . Our young Piony at the foot of the Fir tree has just blown & looks very handsome; & the whole of the Shrubbery Border will soon be very gay with Pinks & Sweet Williams, in addition to the Columbines already in bloom. The Syringas too are coming out.—We are likely to have a great crop of Orleans plumbs—but not many greengages—on the standard scarcely any—three or four dozen perhaps against the wall."[2] The orchard at Chawton sent Jane into Marianne-like ecstasies: "You cannot imagine—it is not in Human nature to imagine what a nice walk we have round the Orchard.—The row of Beech look very well indeed, & so does the young Quickset hedge in the Garden.—I hear today that an Apricot has been detected on one of the trees."[3] One suspects irony in the line "it is not in Human nature to imagine," but ironically or not, Jane paid attention to the garden. There is no irony in her description of the views and grounds of one "Mr Spicer" of Esher: "the views were beautiful. I cannot say what we did *not* see, but I should think there could not be a Wood or a Meadow or a Palace or a remarkable spot in England that was not spread out before us, on one side or the other."[4] She vicariously enjoyed the views of Scotland Henry had seen on his trip there: "I wish he had had more time & could have gone farther north, & deviated to the Lakes in his way back, but what he was able to do seems to have afforded him great Enjoyment & he met with Scenes of higher Beauty in Roxburghshire than I had supposed the South of Scotland possessed."[5]

By the time Austen was in her twenties, English poetry and art veered in a different direction. Romantics disliked the organized symmetry of the eighteenth century, and reveled in the disorganized wildness of the untamed wilderness. Romantic paintings capture sublime, titanic nature, and if human beings appear at all they are too small to have any appreciable effect on the world around them. The world is what it is, in all its terrifying energy, and human beings are only a small part of it. Jane saw it coming, and was satirizing Romanticism before Romanticism existed. When Marianne goes into ecstasies over autumn leaves, her sensible sister Elinor replies, "Not everyone shares your passion for *dead* leaves."

Though Austen responded to natural beauty, her tastes were too minute to include a love of "nature." She loved England; like Mr. Knightley, she celebrated "English verdure, English culture, English comfort," but even "England" was not particular enough. England was too expansive a thing to love. She loved the meadows and wooded hills, the comfortable houses and clear-running streams, the elm groves and the hedgerows that surrounded her in her early years. She loved Hampshire.

In 1800, suddenly, she was cut off from her beloved landscape. While Jane and Cassandra were visiting the Lloyds at Ibthorpe, Mr. and Mrs. Austen abruptly decided to move the remaining family—parents and two adult daughters—to Bath:

> His daughters came home to be met by their mother. "Well girls!" she said abruptly, "it is all settled; we have decided to leave Steventon and go to Bath." Overcome by shock, Jane fainted dead away. This reaction is unlike anything else related of her and, for that reason, very revealing. It shows how overwhelmingly strong was a love of home and countryside that could compel her to a display of emotion so contrary to the habits of a lifetime.[6]

Caroline remembered that Jane opposed to the move from Steventon: "My Aunts had been away a little while, and were met in the Hall on their return by their Mother who told them it was settled, and they were going to live at Bath. My Mother who was present said my Aunt Jane was greatly distressed—All things were done in a hurry by Mr. Austen."[7] Mrs. Austen was, or believed herself to be, in poor health, and Bath promised abundant remedies and a physician on every corner. Mrs. Austen also hoped that moving closer to her wealthy relatives— the Leigh-Perrots and the more distantly related Lady Saye and Sele—might stand her in good stead for a future inheritance. With Jane in her midtwenties and fast approaching irrecoverable spinsterhood, her parents may have aimed to put her in closer contact with eligible young (or older) men.[8] Whatever the reasons, George Austen rapidly settled his affairs—providing for the curacy of Steventon, ending his lease on the farm in Cheesedown, arranging for the sale of his household and farm goods—and moved the family into the city.[9]

Bath was one of the places to be in eighteenth-century England, the baths a destination for the ailing and the whole city a tourist trap boasting England's most ostentatious display of Georgian taste in architecture, consumerism, and city planning. A foreign visitor, Louis Simond, described the city after a visit in 1810:

> [Bath] is certainly beautiful. It is built of freestone, of a fine cream-colour, and contains several public edifices, in good taste. We remarked a circular place called the Crescent, another called the Circus; all the streets straight and regular. This town looks as if it had been cast in a mould all at once; so new, so fresh, so regular. . . . Bath is a sort of great monastery, inhabited by single people, particularly superannuated females. No trade, no manufactures, no occupations of any sort, except that of killing time, the most laborious of

all. Half of the inhabitants do nothing, the other half supply them with nothings: multitude of splendid shops, full of all that wealth and luxury can desire, arranged with all the arts of seduction.[10]

Jane's initial impression of the city was not so enthusiastic. "The first view of Bath in fine weather," she wrote to Cassandra, "does not answer my expectations; I think I see more distinctly thro' Rain.—The Sun was got behind everything, and the appearance of the place from the top of Kingsdown, was all vapour, shadow, smoke & confusion."[11]

Though shaken by the move, Jane rapidly decided to make the best of it: "We have lived long enough in this neighbourhood, the Basingstroke Balls are certainly on the decline, there is something interesting in the bustle of going away, and the prospect of spending future summers by the sea or in Wales is very delightful." She joked that her sacrifice of familiar territory gave her a heroic status similar to that of the wives of sailors and soldiers "which I have often thought of with envy": "It must not be generally known however that I am not sacrificing a great deal in quitting the country—or I can expect to inspire no tenderness, no interest in those we leave behind."[12]

Initially, she found the variety of Bath diverting. She settled with her parents at No. 4 Sydney Place, and later at Green Park Buildings in the older part of the city. She visited the famous Pump House (a central location in *Northanger Abbey*) and other public locations, and inspected the locals. She detailed the fashions to Cassandra, and described all the family's new acquaintances with characteristic shrewdness and blunt insight.

An admirer named Evelyn took her for rides in his phaeton: "I really believe he is very harmless," she assured Cassandra. "People do not seem afraid of him here and he gets groundsel for his birds and all that."[13] She caught a glimpse of the scandalous Mary Cassandra Twisleton, whose husband had divorced her after an affair:

> I am proud to say that I have a very good eye at an Adulteress, for tho' repeatedly assured that another in the party was *she*, I fixed upon the right one from the first. A resemblance to Mrs Leigh was my guide. She is not so pretty as I expected; her face has that same defect of baldness as her sister's, and her features are not so handsome; she was highly rouged, and looked rather quietly and contentedly silly than anything else.[14]

Mr. and Mrs. Austen enjoyed Bath thoroughly, and Mr. Austen—whose wavy hair had turned a brilliant white and whose piercing eyes had lost none of their intensity—captured attention whenever he ventured onto the streets of the city.[15] Austen realized that Bath served as a neat representative of her age, and she set two novels—*Northanger Abbey* and *Persuasion*—partly in that city.

Change of location was not the only disruption in Austen's life at this time. During a holiday in the seaside resort of Sidmouth, Devonshire, she met a young man who fancied her and caught her attention as well. Nothing is known of him for certain, though family lore determined he was a clergyman. He was called away from Sidmouth, promising to return and rejoin the Austens, but they soon received news of his death. No letters from the following months remain, and one can only speculate on the real relation between Austen and this mysterious maybe-lover. Years later, Caroline recorded what she learned from Cassandra about the incident. Jane met a "very charming young man," and

> I never heard Aunt Cass. speak of anyone else with such admiration—she had no doubt that a mutual attachment was in progress between him and her sister. They parted—but he made it plain that he should seek them out again—& shortly afterwards he died!—My Aunt told me this in the late years of her own life—&it was quite new to me then—but all this, being nameless and dateless, cannot I know serve any purpose of your's—and it brings no contradiction to your theory that she Aunt Jane never *had* any attachment that overclouded her happiness, for long. *This* had not gone far enough, to leave any misery behind.[16]

In 1802, Austen's romantic life received another jolt. Visiting the Biggs sisters at Manydown, twenty-one-year-old Harris Bigg-Wither—big, stuttering, unwell[17]—proposed to Jane, who was six years older. Jane had known the family for many years, and considered Harris a decent man in a family she loved and enjoyed. She accepted his proposal, which likely did not come as a surprise, but by the following morning she thought the better of it and reversed her decision. Her niece Catherine Hubback later said that "it was in a momentary fit of self-delusion that she Aunt Jane accepted Mr. Wither's proposal, and that when it was all settled eventually, and the negative decisively given she was much relieved—I think the affair vexed her a good deal—but I am sure she had no attachment to him."[18] David Cecil takes her change of mind as evidence that she was still attached to her Sidmouth lover,[19] and Claire Harman believes her refusal to be evidence that she was reluctant to part with the freedom to write that singleness offered. Perhaps she was simply, in all charity, sparing future generations of English literature students from having to read the works of "Jane Bigg-Wither."

One of the benefits of the move to Bath was the prospect of visiting the coast and viewing the sea that her brothers were sailing. In 1803, the Austens visited Lyme, in Dorset, for a seaside holiday, and Jane had the opportunity to go sea-bathing in an odd eighteenth-century bathhouse contraption. Jane remembered the area vividly, and later wrote one of her most impassioned descriptive passages about the town:

> A very strange stranger it must be, who does not see charms in the immediate environs of Lyme, to make him wish to know it better. The scenes in its neighbourhood, Charmouth, with its high grounds and extensive sweeps of country, and still more its retired bay, backed by dark cliffs, where fragments of low rock among the sands make it the happiest spot for watching the flow of the tide, for sitting in unwearied contemplation; the woody varieties of the cheerful village of Up Lyme, and above all, Pinny, with its green chasms between romantic rocks, where the scattered forest trees and orchards of luxuriant growth declare that many a generation must

have passed away since the first partial falling of the cliff prepared the ground for such a state, where a scene so wonderful
and so lovely is exhibited, as may more than equal any of
the resembling scenes of the far-famed Isle of Wight: these
places must be visited, and visited again, to make the worth
of Lyme understood.[20]

With its evident delight in the sublime beauty of rocks and cliffs,
its evocation of long-forgotten natural history, its yearning
for "unwearied contemplation," this passage might have been
written by William Wordsworth. It is one of the only golden
passages in Austen.

LOSSES

The ups and downs of Austen's romantic life were slight compared to the double tragedy of the winter of 1804–05. On
December 16, 1804—Jane's birthday—Madam Lefroy died
when a horse bolted and threw her. She hit the ground so hard
that she lost consciousness and never awoke.[21] Jane was still
mourning her death four years later, and wrote a poem on her
birthday in 1808 in memory of her friend and mentor, comparing her to the man Jane thought of as "dear Dr. Johnson."

The day returns again, my natal day;
What mix'd emotions with the Thought arise!
Beloved friend, four years have pass'd away
Since thou wert snatch'd forever from our eyes.—
The day, commemorative of my birth

> Bestowing Life and Light and Hope on me,
> Brings back the hour which was thy last on Earth.
> Oh! bitter pang of torturing Memory!—
> Angelic Woman! past my power to praise
> In Language meet, thy Talents, Temper, mind.
> Thy solid Worth, thy captivating Grace!—
> Thou friend and ornament of Humankind!—
> At Johnson's death by Hamilton 'twas said,
> 'Seek we a substitute—Ah! vain the plan,
> No second best remains to Johnson dead—
> None can remind us even of the Man.'
> So we of thee—unequall'd in thy race
> Unequall'd thou, as he the first of Men.
> Vainly we search around the vacant place,
> We ne'er may look upon thy like again. . . .
> Fain would I feel an union in thy fate,
> Fain would I seek to draw an Omen fair
> From this connection in our Earthly date.
> Indulge the harmless weakness—Reason, spare.—

Less than a month later, the family suffered a more dev-astating loss. Jane's father died on January 2, 1805, from an illness that lasted only forty-eight hours. It fell to Jane to send the news to her brother Frank, serving as a naval captain aboard the HMS *Leopard*. "It has been very sudden!" she wrote:

> within twenty four hours of his death he was walking with only the help of a stick, was even reading!—We had how-ever some hours of preparation, & when we understood his

> recovery to be hopeless, most fervently did we pray for the
> speedy release with ensued. To have seen him languishing
> long, struggling for Hours, would have been dreadful!—&
> thank God! we were all spared from it. Except the restlessness
> & confusion of high fever, he did not suffer.

She took comfort, as she frequently did, in the ease of his death, and his lifelong preparation as a believing Christian: "Heavy as is the blow, we can already feel that a thousand comforts remain to us to soften it. Next to that of the consciousness of his worth & constant preparation for another World, is the remembrance of his having suffered, comparatively speaking, nothing.— Being quite insensible of his own state, he was spared all the pain of separation, & he went off almost in his sleep." She reminisced of her father's "virtuous and happy life," and praised his "tenderness as a Father." His corpse did him justice: "It preserves the sweet, benevolent smile which always distinguished him."[22]

With the death of Rev. Austen, Mrs. Austen and her daughters were instantly deprived of most of their livelihood. George left an inheritance that would produce 210£ a year, not enough to support three adult women. Jane's brothers pitched in quickly. James and Henry promised 50£ per year, Edward chipped in another 100, and Frank also offered to send 100 a year. Frank could not afford it, and at Mrs. Austen's insistence his contribution was reduced to 50£. Henry described his mother's reaction to the Austen boys' generosity in a letter to Frank: "It was so absolutely necessary that your noble offer toward Mother should be made more public than you seem'd to desire, that I really cannot apologize for a partial breach of your request. With the proudest exultations of maternal tenderness the Excellent Parent has exclaimed that never were Children so good as hers."[23] Jane was deprived of a father, and also of her most enthusiastic literary advocate. He combined good literary taste with practical worldly sense in a way that few others could.

It is commonly thought that these disruptions interrupted Austen's literary career for the better part of a decade, creating caesura between the early novels of her twenties and the published work of her midthirties. Cassandra's catalog of the dates of her sister's work contributes to this impression, with its gap between the beginning of *Sense and Sensibility* in November 1797 and the beginning of *Mansfield Park* in February 1811. Yet Claire Harman is surely right to say that "it's hard to imagine how the author of 'First Impressions' and "Elinor and Marianne' could have borne to leave them festering in drawer year after year."[24] Austen ended the eighteenth century with three manuscripts and a collection of comic *Juvenalia*. None of it had been published. Her work over the following decade is obscure; we know that she wrote *The Watsons* in 1804, but laid it aside unfinished. In all likelihood, she also continued to perfect her existing three novels, "lop't and crop't" away, and it is entirely possible that she wrote and discarded other work.

When the Crosby publishing company failed year after year to publish her "Susan" (*Northanger Abbey*), Austen wrote under the name Mrs. Ashton Dennis to inquire after it, signing the letter with the initials MAD. This was in April 1809, when, by conventional accounts, Jane had given up her writing career.[25] Moving, death, anxieties about money and the future must have hampered Jane's writing to some degree, but that she ceased writing for a decade is scarcely conceivable.

I LIKE PEWTER TOO

In the years after Rev. Austen's death, the Austen women moved several times. They left their home in 3 Green Park, Bath, to cheaper accommodations at 25 Gay Street, and nine months later moved again to Trim Street, in the center of Bath. In July 1806, they moved from Bath for good, visiting their Leigh relatives at Adlestrop before settling in Southampton, where Frank had recently set up house with his wife Mary. They stayed with Frank for the last months of 1806, then took a house of their own in Castle Square in Southampton, wanting to relieve Frank of the responsibility of caring for them in addition to his growing family.[26]

According to William Gilpin, "Southampton is an elegant, well-built town. It stands on the confluence of two larger waters; and when the tide is full, is seated on a peninsula. It is a town of great antiquity, and still preserves its respectable appendages of ancient walls and gates. The country around is beautiful."[27] When they moved from Frank's home, they took an old house in Castle Square, which butted up against the ancient city walls. From the walkway on top of the wall, Jane could gaze out across a strip of sea to the Isle of Wight.[28] Jane was not disappointed to leave Bath. It no longer held the fascination it once had, and Southampton was an improvement. It was in Hampshire for one thing, and near the sea for another.

Southampton placed the Austen women within easy reach of the other Austen men. James, now installed in his father's former position as rector at Steventon, was close enough to visit regularly, and Edward had property in Hampshire that he would visit occasionally. Jane and Cassandra were both regular guests at his estate at Godmersham.

Life was not easy. Jane had always been conscious of money. "Tho' I like praise as well as anybody," she wrote to Cassandra, "I like what Edward calls *Pewter* too." Particularly when visiting Bath or other cities, she noted prices for meat, butter, cheese, fish, as well as silk, cotton, and articles of clothing.[29] Later, she carefully tracked the income she received from her published works,[30] joking to Cassandra, "I am very rich."[31] At times, especially after her father's death, Austen went beyond carefulness to anxiety about money.[32] Her apparent obsession with money was enough to make the poet W. H. Auden "uncomfortable to see / An English spinster of the middle-class" who could "reveal so frankly and with such sobriety / the economic basis of society."

With her father's death, Austen, along with her sister and her mother, suddenly found herself in a situation not unlike that of her characters, whose simple lack of income is often compounded by mean selfishness of others. At the beginning of *Sense and Sensibility*, John Dashwood intends to bestow 1000*l* on each of his half sisters, which is not much but enough to provide some income. However, his wife, Fanny, convinces him that they would impoverish their own son if they gave so much to the girls, and John, worn down, finally concludes: "I am convinced within myself that your father had no idea of your giving them any money at all." Jane may have been writing in part from experience. Godmersham was not entirely a happy place for Jane. Edward's wife was not fond of Jane, too clever and perhaps too low-class for a noble estate. According to Anna Lefroy, "A little talent went a long way with the Goodneston Bridgeses of that period; & *much* must have gone a long way too far."[33]

Austen was concerned not only about the effect that relative poverty has on the marital fortunes of her characters but also with the way money and luxury, or poverty and deprivation, reveals and shapes character. She knew that consumption is not only about purchasing goods but also about identity. For Austen, syntax is character; spending is character too, and she never approves of extravagance, especially heavy spending on oneself. Mr. Knightley is an ideal. He has great estates, and manages them himself; he could be a wastrel rich boy, but instead he oversees his operations with thrift, prudence, and, above all, generosity. Robert Ferrars is at the opposite extreme. He keeps everyone waiting at a shop as he selects just the right toothpick case, and this shows that the "correctness of his eye, and the delicacy of his taste" are greater than the really important thing, his "politeness."

During this period, the Austen women visited Mrs. Austen's cousin Thomas Leigh at the ancestral property of Stoneleigh Abbey, "the only occasion, so far as we know, that Jane Austen stayed at a great aristocratic country mansion."[34] Mrs. Austen reveled in its bright spaciousness:

I had expected to find everything about the place very fine and all that, but I had no idea of its being so beautiful. I had pictured myself long avenues, dark rookeries, and dismal yew trees but here are no such dismal things. The Avon runs near the house, amidst green meadows, bounded by large and beautiful woods, full of delightful walks.[35]

She was impressed by the abundance of the life in a great house:

At nine in the morning we say our prayers in a handsome chapel, of which the pulpit, &c. &c is now hung with black. Then follows breakfast, consisting of chocolate, coffee, and tea, plum cake, pound cake, hot rolls, cold rolls, bread and butter, and dry toast for me. . . . The ponds supply excellent fish, the park excellent venison; there is a great quantity of rabbits, pigeons, and all sorts of poultry. There is a delightful dairy, where is made butter, good Warwickshire cheese and cream ditto.[36]

STILL JENNY

The Austens' residence at Southampton was not permanent. After Edward's wife, Elizabeth, died in 1808, Edward, needing feminine assistance nearby, offered his mother and sisters a choice of two homes, one a house on the Godmersham estate in Kent and the other close to Chawton House on his Hampshire property. The Austen women chose the latter, and moved into the Chawton Cottage in July 1809. Jane wrote some verses to Frank for the occasion:

As for ourselves, we're very well

As unaffected prose will tell—.
Cassandra's pen will paint our state
The many comforts that await
Our Chawton home, how much we find
Already in it, to our mind;
And how convinced, that when complete
It will all other Houses beat
that ever have been made or mended
With rooms concise, or rooms distended.[37]

Austen continued to live, as she always had, with her family, taking care of household chores and finding time to write when she could. She got up early to practice the piano, then fixed toast for breakfast. Caroline remembered, "After luncheon, my Aunts generally walked out—sometimes they went to Alton for shopping—Often, one or the other of them, to the Great House—as it was then called—when a brother was inhabiting it, to make a visit—or if the house were standing empty they liked to stroll about the grounds—sometimes to Chawton Park—a noble beech wood, just within a walk—but sometimes, but that was rarely, to call on a neighbor."[38] Aunt Jane "was fond of work—and she was a great adept at overcast and satin stich—the peculiar delight of that day—General handiness and neatness were amongst the characteristics."[39]

According to the writer Mary Russell Mitford, whose mother knew Austen as a girl, Jane Austen was "unbending" and "no more regarded in society than a poker of a fire-screen, or any other thin, upright piece of wood or iron." A friend had told her that as she aged, Jane had "stiffened into the most perpendicular, precise, taciturn piece of 'single blessedness' that ever existed."[40] Perhaps such was the case for Austen's demeanor around strangers, but in the familiar surroundings of her family, she remained Jenny Austen.

Nothing shows this more clearly than her friendships with nieces and nephews. Austen enjoyed the company of children, and children returned the compliment. This may seem surprising, since she never married and had no children of her own. It also surprises because her books contain some of the most brutally funny portraits of bratty children in English literature. When Miss Steele accidentally pricks one of Lady Middleton's children with a hairpin while hugging her, little Annamaria plays it for all its worth:

> The mother's consternation was excessive; but it could not surpass the alarm of the Misses Steele, and every thing was done by all three, in so critical an emergency, which affection could suggest, as likely to assauge the agonies of the little sufferer. She was seated in her mother's lap, covered with kisses, her wound bathed with lavender-water, by one of the Misses Steele, who was on her knees to attend her, and her mouth stuffed with sugar plums by the other. With such a reward for her tears, the child was too wise to cease crying. She still screamed and sobbed lustily, kicked her two brothers for offering to touch her: and all their united soothings were ineffectual, till Lady Middleton, luckily remembering that in a scene of similar distress last week some apricot marmalade had been successfully applied for a bruised temple, the same remedy was eagerly proposed for this unfortunate

scratch, and a slight intermission of screams in the young lady on hearing it, gave them reason to hope that it would not be rejected.[41]

The only sympathy for the child comes from the characters. The narrator shows none. We can almost hear her whisper, "The brat deserves all she gets" as Jenny, acting as if she were still thirteen, gleefully sticks her fictional pin into a fictional child.

Jane sometimes seems to be fantasizing about sticking pins in real children. Edward's children could be trying. "Mary finds the Children less troublesome than she expected," she informed Cassandra during a visit to Edward's Kent estate, "& independent of them, there is certainly not much to try the patience or hurt the Spirits at Godmersham."[42] She admitted to writing with "a little bitterness" about her nephews, though she took some hope in observing "that they were both at the Sacrament yesterday." She worried that they would disappoint her again: "these two Boys who are out with the Foxhounds will come home & disgust me again by some habit of Luxury of some proof of sporting Mania—unless I keep it off by this prediction."[43] As ever, criticism of her nephews was softened by her comic exaggerations. At the birth of Frank's second son, Henry, she expressed to Cassandra the "hope if he ever comes to be hanged, it will not be till we are too old to care about it."[44]

Austen occasionally expressed pity for women who were continuously pregnant. In 1808, she heard that Frances Tilson, wife of Henry Austen's banking partner, was pregnant: "poor Woman! how can she be honestly breeding again?"[45] Five years later, Mrs. Tilson was as "affectionate and pleasing as ever," but "from her appearance I suspect her to be in the family way. Poor Woman! Fanny prophecies the Child's coming in 3 or 4 days."[46] When it was all said and done, poor "Mrs. T," as Austen called her, had "at least eleven children."[47] Several of her brothers were equally prolific. James had three children by two wives—Anna, James-Edward, and Caroline-Mary-Craven. Edward had eleven (six sons, five daughters) before his wife died shortly after the last birth, in 1808. Francis also had eleven, and the same proportion of boys and girls as Edward (six sons, five daughters). Austen became particularly close to James's eldest, Anna, and also to Edward's eldest, , Fanny.

Despite misgivings about perpetual breeding, she rejoiced in her brothers' progeny, and she had a great deal of progeny to rejoice about. When Frank's wife, Mary, had the couple's first son, Francis-William, in July 1809, Aunt Jane celebrated the event by sending Frank a poem:

> My dearest Frank, I wish you Joy
> Of Mary's safety with a boy,
> Whose birth has given little pain,
> Compared with that of Mary Jane. –
> May he a growing blessing prove,
> And well deserve his Parents Love!

She expressed the hope that Francis-William would grow up to be a man of his father's caliber:

> In Manhood shew his Father's mind,

> Like him considerate & kind;
> All Gentleness to those around,
> And eager only not to wound.
> Then like his Father too, he must,
> Fell his Deserts with honest Glow,
> And all his Self-improvement know.[48]

Anna remembered Jane as a "general favorite with children." She was "playful" and her stories "delightful": "These were continued from time to time, & begged for of course at all possible or impossible occasions; woven, as she proceeded out of nothing but her own happy talent for invention. Ah! If but one of them could be now recovered!"[49] For Caroline, "Her charm to children was great sweetness of manner—she seemed to love you, and you loved her naturally in return." Caroline remembered her aunt as an affectionate and accessible woman: "Aunt Jane was the great charm—As a very little girl, I was always creeping up to her, and following her whenever I *could*, *in* the house and out of it—I might not have remembered *this*, but for the recollection of my Mother's telling me privately, I must not be troublesome to my Aunt."[50] She added,

> Everything she could make amusing to a child—Then, as I got older, and when cousins came to share the entertainment, she would tell us the most delightful stories chiefly of Fairyland, and her Fairies had all characters of their own— The tale was invented, I am sure, at the moment, and was sometimes continued for 2 or 3 days, if occasion served.[51]

Of Jane's letters to her, she recalled that "Aunt Jane was so good as frequently to write to *me*; and in addressing a child, she was perfect."

Jane played games with her nieces and nephews: "*She* could throw the spilikens for us, better than anyone else, and she was wonderfully successful at cup and ball—She found a resources sometimes in that simple game, when she suffered from weak eyes and could not work or read for long together."[52] One day at Godmersham Mrs. Austen, Jane, Cassandra, and some assorted household servants "played at school" with the children, Cassandra taking the part of "Mrs Teachum the Governness" and Jane "Miss Popham the Teacher." All "dressed in Character and we had a most delightful day."[53] When the ten-year-old daughter of one of Frank's friends visited Chawton, Jane opened "the Treasures of my Writing-desk drawer" to keep her amused, and found her "a nice, natural, openhearted, affectionate girl, with all the ready civility which one sees in the best Children of the present day."[54] On another visit to Godmersham, a thirty-year-old Jane spent a day writing to Frank and "playing at Battledore and Shuttlecock with William," her seven-year-old nephew.[55] With the girls, Aunt Jenny provided dress-up clothes and played house:

> [We] often had amusements in which my Aunt was very helpful—She was one to whom we always looked for help—She would furnish us with what we wanted from her wardrobe, and she would often be the entertaining visitor in our make beleive house—She amused us in various ways— *once* I remember in giving a conversation as between myself

and my two cousins, supposed to be grown up, the day after
a Ball.[56]

James Edward "did not think of her as being clever, still less as
being famous," but with his cousins "valued her as one always
kind, sympathizing, and amusing."[57]

Edwards's sons were not at home at Godmersham when
their mother died, and Jane was with them when a letter brought
the news. "George sobbed aloud, Edward's tears did not flow so
easily," but both understood the import of what had happened.
Remembering from watching her brothers how boys amuse
themselves, Austen spent the next several days distracting her
nephews with games: "We do not want amusement; bilbocatch,
at which George is indefatigable, spillikins, paper ships, riddles,
conundrums, and cards, with watching the flow and ebb of the
river, and now and then a stroll out, keep us well employed."[58] It
was one of Aunt Jane's shining moments, an act of sympathetic
condescension when she became like the boys to minister to the
boys, when she became a child to comfort children.

She was slow to give up youthful amusements as well. Even
as she approached thirty, Jenny continued to attend dances,
long after she had lost hope of securing a husband. Though
conscious of being "so much older" than the other women,
she sounded like a schoolgirl as she boasted to Cassandra,
"You will not expect to hear that I was asked to dance—but I
was—by the Gentleman whom we saw *that Sunday* with Captn
D'auvergne."[59] Austen never lost the instinct to adopt poses,
which she ironically knew to be poses. She attended the theater
to see Don Juan, "whom we left in Hell at ? past 11."[60] One

home was full of "modern Elegancies," but lacked an air of seriousness: "if it had not been for some naked Cupids over the Mantlepiece, which must be a fine study for Girls, one should never have Smelt Instruction."[61] The wit is layered here—the irony of girls staring at naked male cupids as an art lesson, the suggestion that instruction is something to be "smelt," the mock-pompous capitalization of "Smelt Instruction" that A. A. Milne turned into a stock joke.

She was also full of affectionate mockery toward Cassandra. *Pride and Prejudice*, she suggested, should include some digressions on important subjects to add "shade" to the "light & bright & sparkling" atmosphere, but she doubted that Cassandra would agree: "I know your starched Notions."[62] She closed one letter with the claim that she had evened up her letter writing: "My ideas of Justice in Epistolary Matters are you know very strict."[63] Much of her playful mockery is directed at herself. Reading a book on the British Empire by one Captain Pasley, she confided, "I am as much in love with the author as I ever was with Clarkson or Buchanan . . . the first soldier I ever sighed for; but he does write with extraordinary force and spirit."[64]

One of her favorite poses—and it is certainly not entirely a pose—is that of misanthrope. She confided to Cassandra that she did "not want People to be very agreeable, as it saves me the trouble of liking them a great deal."[65] Her observations on people's looks, behavior, and fashion sometimes border on cruel, and sometimes pass well over the border. One Mrs. Blount "appeared exactly as she did in September, with the same broad face, diamond bandeau, white shoes, pink husband, & fat neck." At the same ball, two Miss Coxes were in attendance, one of them still "the vulgar, broad-featured girl who danced at Enham eight years ago."[66] This is one of Jenny Austen's childish vices—a quickness to point out flaws that polite adults pretend, for the sake of decorum, to overlook.

Much of Austen's adult humor, like her teenage humor, was more silly than witty. It was no accident that she laughed often and heartily with her teenaged nieces. When visiting Godmersham, Aunt Jane would close herself in a room with Fanny so they could read together, leaving the other children wondering at the peals of laughter coming from within.[67] Anna and Aunt Jane read romance novels aloud to make fun of them. During a "summer visit at Chawton" Anna went to get novels at the Alton library, and came back to relate the plots to her aunt: "Greatly we both enjoyed it, one piece of absurdity leading to another," until the more adult Cassandra "fatigued with her own share of laughter [would] exclaim, 'How *can* you both be so foolish.'" One particular novel by "Mrs Hunter" was very long and "in a most unaccountable manner told the same story about the same people, most of whom I think had died before the real story began was repeated 3 or 4 times over." Jane wrote a mock letter to Mrs. Hunter, describing how "Miss Jane Austen's tears have flowed over each sweet sketch in such a way that as would do Mrs Hunter's heart good to see."[68] Jane and Fanny invented a language in which every word began with a *p*, and she informed Fanny through Cassandra that an art exhibition at Spring Gardens included a picture of "Mrs. Bingley," the married Jane Bennet from *Pride and Prejudice*. Mrs. Bingley "is dressed in white gown, with green oranaments, which convinces me of what I had always supposed, that green was a favourite colour with her."[69]

She enjoyed teasing her nephew as well. Like his cousin Fanny and half sister Anna, James Edward was an aspiring novelist. When he wrote to Aunt Jane lamenting the loss of two and a half chapters of a manuscript he was working on, Jane replied, "It is well that I have not been at Steventon lately, & therefore cannot be suspected of purloining them;—two strong twigs and a half towards a Nest of my own, would have been something."[70] She worried about scandalous reports she expected to hear concerning his visit to Winchester:

> Now you may own, how miserable you were there; now, it will gradually all come out—your Crimes & your Miseries— how often you went up by the Mail to London and threw away Fifty Guineas at a Tavern, & how often you were on the point of hanging yourself—restrained only, as some ill-natured aspersion upon some poor old Winton has it, by the want of a Tree within some miles of the City.[71]

To her niece Cassandra, daughter to brother Charles, she wrote an entire letter in which every word is spelled backward. "I hsiw uoy a yppah wen raey," she began, and closed, after a bit of family news, with "Tnua Ardnassac sdnes reh tseb evol, dna os ew od lla."[72] To Cassandra, she wrote garbled reports about brother Frank: "Frank has rec:d his appointment on Board the Captn John Gore commanded by the Triton."[73] In one letter, she tires of writing, and declares, "I am going to write nothing but short Sentences." And for three and a half more pages she writes fragmentary thoughts that remind us of *Emma's* Mrs. Elton.[74]

Even as she approached and passed the age of thirty, even as she stiffened into middle-age propriety, Jane's laughter remained that of a fifteen-year-old, the laughter of Jenny Austen, the laughter that filled her letters and provided the pulse of her novels.

PUBLISHED AUTHOR

Only a woman of more than ordinary determination could have finished six novels, started two more, and left behind three volumes of juvenile writing in forty-one years. Determination was a trait Jane shared with her family. Few women are more deserving of the title "indomitable" than Mrs. Austen, and Jane grew up surrounded by several competent, accomplished, and determined young men.

We get a rare glimpse of Jane's own form of this family trait, which spills over into competitiveness, in a letter to Cassandra written from the Leigh-Perrots' home at the Paragon, shortly after Jane's move to Bath. She took a walk with one Mrs. Chamberlayne, with whom she was becoming acquainted:

> It would have amused you to see our progress;—we went up by Sion Hill, & returned across the fields;—in climbing a hill Mrs. Chamberlayne is very capital; I could with difficulty keep pace with her—yet would not flinch for the World.—on plain ground I was quite her equal—and so we posted away

under a fine hot sun, She without any parasol or any shade to her hat, stopping for nothing, & crossing the Church Yard at Weston with as much expedition as if were afraid of being buried alive. After seeing what she is equal to, I cannot help feeling a regard for her.[1]

She "would not flinch for the World." That is the voice of a woman who continued writing even after all her efforts at publication were frustrated, and kept writing until she had written herself a place in every literary canon in the world.

The delays in publication must have rankled. Samuel Egerton Brydges's books got published and sold briskly enough, and Austen was confident enough of her own gifts to know that she was vastly better than Egerton. No doubt, she was pleased that her books delighted the members of her family, but she also wanted a wider readership and, conscious of money as she always was, especially after her father's death in 1805, she hoped that book sales would allow her to contribute to the support of the Austen women.[2] She oftentimes became gripped by the fear that she would end up like her brother James, the talented poet of the family whose latter years were marked by the lethargic bitterness of unrealized ambition.

Delay had its advantages. "The longer Austen remained unpublished," Claire Harman observes, "the more experimental she became, and the more license she assumed with bold, brilliant moves."[3] Had she published earlier, her novels might have settled into predictable conventions. Further, because she continued rewriting the novels first written in her twenties, Jane lived with her characters longer than most authors, and that gave her time to "love them and fantasise about them," so that her "long-held control over her texts is one of the things that generates the unusual feeling of *life going on* in them."[4] Austen grasped the advantage of unpublished anonymity, writing to Cassandra that, while she was gratified that her niece Fanny Knight liked her writing, "I wish the knowledge of my being exposed to her discerning Criticism, may not hurt my stile, by introducing too great a solicitude." She noticed that she was already beginning "to weight my words & sentences more than I did, & am looking about for a sentiment, an illustration or a metaphor in every corner of the room."[5]

Advantageous or not, remaining unpublished did not appeal to Austen. She wanted to move past her phase of private novel writing, and from the Chawton Cottage she was able to launch her career as an author. The Chawton Cottage lay in the curve of the road where the road forks, left to Chawton Park and right to Winchester.

> A timber-framed house which had since been clad in red brick, the cottage had an air of great solidity and squareness, but without that perfect symmetry indicative of Georgian origin. It was evidently an older building which had been improved and altered over the years, in a somewhat piecemeal fashion, but it was no less comfortable and charming for that. Only the front windows were sash; the little casements remained at the back, which sprawled away into a collection of outbuildings, including a room which doubled as a bakehouse and wash-house. There were six bedchambers, none of them large, and two garret windows pierced the roof.[6]

From the mahogany desk purchased by her father in a house set so close to the London-Winchester road that she could gaze out the parlor window to see the occupants of the passing carriages, the thirty-something Jane Austen launched a literary career.

How it happened is, characteristically, obscure. There are no surviving letters from 1810, and when Jenny re-emerged in the sources in the spring of 1811 she was sending off the manuscript of *Sense and Sensibility* to the London publisher Thomas Egerton, a publishing deal already made. Henry acted as her literary agent, and when the proofs arrived, Jane went to visit her brother and Eliza at their home on Sloane Street in London. In her spare time, she shopped, one destination being the shop of the famous china producer Josiah Wedgewood. She did not enjoy shopping, though. She described her excursions as "commissions" she performed for others, and complained about having to wait a "full half an hour" at a "thronged" counter before she could buy some Bugle Trimming and three pairs of silk stockings. Jane enjoyed the more varied social circle in which Henry and Eliza moved, but her trip was primarily for the purpose of doing final corrections. *Sense and Sensibility* was published at the end of October 1811. The following year, she finished revising *Pride and Prejudice*, and it was advertised and published in January 1813.

She hid her authorship from all but the closest of her relatives, for the title page of *Sense and Sensibility* said the book was "By a Lady" and *Pride and Prejudice* "By the Author of *Sense and Sensibility*." Even her niece Anna knew nothing of it. Shortly after its publication:

[t]he two of them [Anna and Jane], looking at the novels in

the Alton Circulating Library, saw *Sense and Sensibility* lying
on the counter. Anna picked up the first volume. "It must be
nonsense with a title like that," she said and put it back again.
Jane watched her amused and silent.[7]

By the time *Pride and Prejudice* was released, she had
already started *Mansfield Park*, which she finished by the summer of 1813 and published the following year. She began writing
Emma in late 1813, and finished it by the early months of 1814.
Between her move to Chawton in 1809 and 1814, she rewrote
or finished rewriting two novels, wrote two more, apparently
from scratch, and published all four. She had already written
Pride and Prejudice as *First Impressions* during the 1790s, and
Sense and Sensibility was also a revision of an earlier work. She
"lop't and crop't" *Pride and Prejudice*, and no doubt had done
the same with *Sense and Sensibility*. Austen's literary career
looks as if it took off in her thirties, but the publication of her
novels was the culmination of her youthful apprenticeship, to
which she added the fresh inspiration of several new projects.

Mansfield Park has been regarded as Austen's most complex
and profound novels. Its main character, Fanny Price, is not as
immediately likeable as Elizabeth or Jane Bennet or Marianne
and Elinor Dashwood. Fanny is mousy, retiring, and shy; and
matters are worse because she is badly out of place, displaced
from her poor and crowded family home to Mansfield Park,
where her mother's sister is the lady of the house. Edmund
Bertram, the heir of Mansfield Park, is kind to Fanny, but she is
bullied by Edmund's sisters and by another aunt, Mrs. Norris.
Two visitors from London, the brother-sister pair Henry and

Mary Crawford, bring a dazzling and seductive new force into the Park, and Mary tries to entice Edmund away from his plans to seek ordination. Despite her apparent weakness, Fanny shows moral strength that ultimately wins Edmund's admiration and love. Faced with a choice between the seductive Mary Crawford and the upright and pious Fanny Price, Edmund chooses Fanny.

Critical of her own work as she was of other authors', Jane was on the whole satisfied with her "children." She was more fulsome on *Pride and Prejudice* than *Sense and Sensibility*. Harriet Benn visited Chawton in January 1813, dining with the Austens the very day the book was released. Jane maintained her anonymity as she and her mother read the first half of Book 1 to their unsuspecting friend. Harriet was amused, but she had little chance to form her own opinion, "with two such people to lead the way." Mrs. Austen read too quickly for Jane's liking,[8] but much to Jane's satisfaction, Harriet admired Elizabeth Bennet: "I must confess that I think her as delightful a creature as ever appeared in print, & how I shall be able to tolerate those who do not like *her* at least, I do not know."[9]

Jane found some errors in the typesetting. In Book 3, page 220, "two speeches are made into one,"[10] and she realized that "a 'said he' or a 'said she' would sometimes make the Dialogue more immediately clear," but added that her readers could figure it out: "I do not write for such dull Elves," alluding to a line from Walter Scott's epic poem *Marmion* ("I do not rhyme to that dull elf,/ Who cannot imagine to himself,/ That all through Flodden's dismal night,/ Wilton was foremost in the fight"). More playfully, she suggested that the book was too "light & bright & sparkling" and needed some grave digressions on important subjects to give it "shade." Yet her sheer delight in the book is evident even in her plans to maintain her secrecy about writing it: "you must be prepared," she instructed Cassandra, "for the Neighbourhood being perhaps already informed of there being such a Work in the World, & in the Chawton World!"[11]

Now that she had published, she wrote self-mockingly about her own ambition. When Cassandra praised her letter-writing skills, she responded, "I write only for Fame, and without any view to pecuniary Emoulment."[12] She spoke in mock praise of her skill: "Expect a most agreeable Letter," she had written to Cassandra, "for not being overburdened with subject—(having nothing at all to say)—I shall have no check to my Genius from beginning to end."[13] She was disappointed that her brother Edward did not like some verses she had written: "they seemed to me purely classical—just like Homer & Virgil, Ovid and Propria que Maribus."[14]

Sense and Sensibility went to a second edition, and Austen surprised herself by earning 140*l* from it,[15] and the first edition of *Mansfield Park* sold out within a year of its publication. Jane began keeping a log of the opinions of friends and critics, and they were largely favorable. One Lady Bessborough wrote to her lover that *Sense and Sensibility* was "a clever novel," though she thought it ended "stupidly."[16] Charles wrote to his sister that *Pride and Prejudice* was popular among his friends in the British navy, and favorable comments came in from the poet Sheridan, Warren Hastings, and Miss Milbanke, the future Lady Byron.[17]

LITTLE MATTERS

Jane's cover of anonymity was slipping, owing to Henry's gregarious nature. On a trip to Scotland, he could not help boasting that his sister was the author of *Pride and Prejudice*:

> A thing once set going in that way! One knows how it spreads . . . I know it is all done from affection and partiality—but at the same time let me here again express to you and Mary my sense of the superior kindness which you have shewn on the occasion in doing what I wished.[18]

Though Henry bragged to his friends about his sister's success, in his biographical note, he emphasized her own modesty as a writer: "In composition she was equally rapid and correct," yet she had "an invincible distrust of her own judgment" and this caused her to withhold works from public "till time and many perusals had satisfied her that the charm of recent composition was dissolved." She never sought literary fame but "became an authoress entirely from taste and inclination. Neither the hope of fame nor profit mixed with her early motives." In fact, when her first book went to publication, "she actually made a reserve from her moderate income to meet the expected loss" and was astonished that *Sense and Sensibility* made 150£. She did not cultivate the life of an author. Though "in the bosom of her family she talked to them freely; thankful for the praise, open to remark, and submissive to criticism," yet "in public she turned away from any allusion to the character of an authoress." Her letters were as finished as her published work: "Every thing came finished from her pen; for on all subjects she had ideas as clear as her expressions were well chosen. It is not too much to say that she never dispatched a note or letter unworthy of publication."[19]

Like many of Henry's reminiscences of his sister, this one seems suspect. Jenny was joking when she told Cassandra she was looking for praise and fame, but her irony serves as a veil that covers and softens real ambition. Had Jane Austen been content with writing for her family, or writing for nothing, she would never have sought publication in the first place. Still, Henry was onto something: There is something profoundly humble about Austen's novels, her career, her style. Humility characterized her work because it characterized Jane herself.

Ambitious as she may have been to be published, she showed no interest in working her way into a literary elite. She once had an opportunity to visit a literary meeting in London, which included the notorious Madame de Stael. Born in Switzerland, Madame de Stael had published numerous books in various genres—novels, essays, drama, political pamphlets—and was praised by her contemporaries as one of the great talents of the age, credited with being the founder of French Romanticism. Austen refused the invitation, protesting that "such a display would have given pain instead of pleasure."[20]

Jane considered herself and her sister to be part of a dying breed. One Mrs. Col. Tilson, she confided to Cassandra, must have been an "alarming Bride," and Jane could discern no purpose in her marriage beyond the bride's desire "to *attract* notice." Such a marriage "announces not *great* sense, & therefore ensures boundless Influence."[21] She couldn't understand the self-promotion. "What is become of all the Shyness in the World?" she asked rhetorically in an 1807 letter. "Moral as well as Natural Diseases disappear in the progress of time, & new ones take their place.—Shyness & the Sweating Sickness have given way to Confidence & Paralytic complaints."

In the grand scheme of things, she recognized her books were trivial. Speaking of *Pride and Prejudice*, she said, "[W]hat a trifle it is in all its Bearings, to the really important points of one's existence even in this World!"[22] Her humility is evident in her attention to "little matters," both in her fiction and in her life. She admitted to their triviality: "I am extremely foolish in writing all this unnecessary stuff," she confessed to Cassandra. Yet, she felt that her letter could not hold all the matters she needed to write about: "Little Matters they are to be sure, but highly important," she wrote, and then she launched into a litany of gossip and unnecessary particulars—the arrival of Miss Curling to Portsmouth, her bracelets, a visit from Mrs. Dickens and her "Sisterinlaw," and so on and on.[23] Austen could hardly examine a room without estimating its dimensions, and she could not describe a pair of silk stockings or a bit of fabric without recording its price. When Edward purchased a pair of Coach Horses, it was not enough to give the fact itself. She had to inform Cassandra, "His friend M Evelyn has all his life thought more of Horses than of anything else.—Their Colour is black & their size not large—their price sixty Guineas, of which the Chair Mare was taken as fifteen—but this is of course to be a secret."[24] Typically, it was not enough to tell Cassandra that Bath women wore flowers and fruit on their hats; she enumerated the fruit: "Eliz: has a bunch of strawberries, & I have seen Grapes, Cherries, Plubs, & Apricots—There are likewise Almonds & raisins, French plumbs and Tamarinds at the Grocers, but I have never seen any of them in hats.—A plumb or a green gage would cost three shillings;—Cherries & Grapes about 5 I believe—but this is at some of the dearest Shops."[25] While still living in her first home, her parents received some tables, which Jane examined carefully: "I had not expected that they would so perfectly suit the fancy of us all three, or that we should so well agree on the disposition of them; but nothing except their own surface can have been smoother;—The two ends put together form our constant Table for everything, & the centre piece stands exceedingly well under the glass; holds a great deal most comodiously, without looking awkwardly.—They are both covered with green baize & send their best Love."[26]

When James Clarke suggested that she write a romance story, she protested her limitations: "I could no more write a romance than an epic poem. I could not sit down to write a serious romance under any other motive than to save my life; and if it were indispensable for me to keep it up and never relax into laughing at myself or other people, I am sure I should be hung before I had finished the first chapter."[27] She advised her niece Anna Lefroy, another aspiring writer in the family, to operate within her limits too. Of Anna's characters, Aunt Jane wrote, "Let the Portmans go to Ireland, but as you know nothing of the manners there, you had better not go with them. Stick to *Bath* and the Foresters. There you will be quite at home."[28] "Mrs. F" would not settle near "Sir T. H." unless she had "some other inducement to go there; she ought to have some friend living thereabouts to tempt her." Sir T. H. for his part would never use such a "familiar and inelegant" expression as "Bless my Heart." She commended "the conversation on Genius &c. Mr. St. J.—& Susan both talk in character and very well."[29] She urged Anna to avoid clichés: "Devereaux Forester's being ruined by his Vanity is extremely good; but I wish you would not let him plunge into a 'vortex of Dissipation.' I do not object to the Thing, but I cannot bear the expression;—it is such thorough novel slang—and so old, that I dare say Adam met with it in the first novel he opened."[30] Writing to her nephew James Edward Austen, an aspiring writer, she contrasted his "strong, manly, spirited Sketches, full of Variety & Glow" with her own work on "the little bit (two Inches wide) of Ivory on which I work with so fine a Brush."[31]

When she ventured outside the scope of her daily life in *Persuasion*, she inquired with her brothers to make sure her details were accurate:

Captain Wentworth, like Frank Austen, has distinguished himself in the action of St. Domingo in 1806, yet it is mostly his early years at sea that he talks about. Like Frank, he commanded a battered old ship, but she was *his* ship and he was proud of her: "she was a dear old Asp to me," he says. "She did all I wanted. I knew she would." Jane remembered other things Frank had told her, too: how captains sometimes stole each other's men to make up their own crews (a practice which Admiral Croft condemns in *Persuasion*); how the Admiralty "entertained themselves now and again" by sending men to sea in rotten ships (a practice which Captain Wentworth thinks might easily have been the death of him);

and how senior officers sometimes abused their position and took to buggery (a piece of information Mary Crawford hints at vulgarly in conversation at Mansfield Park: "Certainly, my home at my uncle's brought me acquainted with a circle of Admirals. Of *Rears*, and *Vices*, I saw enough. (Now, do not be suspecting me of a pun, I entreat").

Jane knew from her brothers that "many offers were equally if not more concerned to capture individual ships and thereby obtain prize money."[32] When she described the process of ordination in *Mansfield Park*, she consulted Henry to get the timing right. Her novels normally function according to a calendar of a particular year, a practice that not only gives the stories verisimilitude but also helps her organize her plots. *Emma*'s Mr. Weston had been with the Surrey Militia and had met his wife in Yorkshire in 1795—and in actual fact, the Surrey Militia had been packed off to Yorkshire because of misconduct.[33] Homer nodded, and Austen too. Her brother Edward wrote after reading *Emma*, wondering how the apple trees could be in bloom during strawberry picking: "Jane, I wish you would tell me where you get those apple-trees of yours that come into bloom in July," he teased.[34]

Frequently Austen wrote like a dramatist. She was no tyrannical puppet master, manipulating her characters to make a point, nor was she given to excessive rhetorical flourishes to manipulate the reader. She was not absent from her fiction, but her presence was subtle enough to pay readers her greatest compliment—her confidence that we can figure out what we are supposed to think based on what she tells us. Her narrative style is a humble style, which makes it artistic.

Austen's fiction would never be confused with Flannery O'Connor's. Austen's characters are recognizable as our next-door neighbors, not the misshapen grotesques of O'Connor's American South. Her novels contain no bizarre drownings, no larcenous Bible salesmen, no evangelists for the Church Without Christ, no Oedipal self-blindings. Yet, Austen's aesthetic is remarkably similar to O'Connor's. Like O'Connor, Austen was devoted to the work. She did want to delight and edify her readers, but her first interest was in being true to what she was creating. Her insistent realism may seem neurotic, but O'Connor echoed it when she wrote that the key to creating the work is to stare at the world, stupidly if necessary, in order to get it right. For Austen and O'Connor, right seeing is not only a literary method, but the moral of many of her stories. In *Pride and Prejudice*, the moral issues all depend on learning to see the world as it actually is and not as we might wish it to be. Elizabeth's prejudices cloud her sight, so that she judges neither Mr. Darcy nor Mr. Wickham accurately, while Darcy's pride initially blinds him to Elizabeth's virtues. That Austen intended to emphasize this point is evident in her early title for the book—*First Impressions*.

Walter Scott compared Austen's fiction to the work of Flemish painters, and critics ever since have commented on Austen's mastery of detail. Charlotte Brontë compared her work to that of a Chinese miniaturist; Austen would not have disagreed, though from Brontë it was not a compliment. She wrote disparagingly of the absence of passion, of the "bonny beck," of romantic effusions in Austen's books. But Austen knew what she was doing, including her limitations. As Virginia

Woolf recognized, Austen is the great writer who is the most difficult to catch in the act of greatness.

MY OWN WAY

The proposal scenes in *Pride and Prejudice*—Collins's three-point sermon and Darcy's "I love you against my better judgment"—are among the best known set pieces in Austen's work. But the climactic scene of that novel is even better. Lady Catherine de Bourgh appears unexpectedly at the Bennet home to demand a personal conference with Elizabeth. She has heard rumors—from the Collinses, we are led to surmise—that Darcy intends to propose to Elizabeth again. Lady Catherine will not permit it. Mr. Darcy, she says, cannot lower himself so much, and besides he is already engaged to Lady Catherine's daughter.

Elizabeth's response is equal parts wit and *chutzpah*. When Lady Catherine protests that Darcy is already engaged to her daughter, Elizabeth replies, "Then you have no reason to believe he will propose to me." Lady Catherine's visit to the Bennets, which she says is intended to prevent rumors of a match between Darcy and Elizabeth, will, Elizabeth points out, have the opposite effect: everyone will take Lady Catherine's visit as evidence of an impending engagement. When Lady Catherine insults Elizabeth's family and character, Elizabeth responds with vigor: "I am a gentleman's daughter." The most remarkable feature of this scene is that Elizabeth responds to Lady Catherine without once exceeding the bounds of politeness set by her station in society. Elizabeth speaks her mind with courage, but she does not shout nor rant nor scratch out Lady

Catherine's eyes nor—as Elizabeth and Lady Catherine both do in the recent *Pride and Prejudice and Zombies*—leap around like a ninja. She operates within the bounds of her position, and recognizes Lady Catherine's position, throughout their encounter. She fights, but she fights like a gentlewoman.

Jane Austen shared Elizabeth's ability to defuse opposition with jolly firmness. When Mrs. Knight suggested that Jane marry Mr. Papillon, who was living in the Chawton rectory, Jane wrote acidly to Cassandra, "I am very much obliged to Mrs. Knight for such a proof of the interest she takes in me—& she may depend upon it, that I will marry Mr. Papillon, whatever may be his reluctance or my own.—I owe her much more than such a trifling sacrifice."[35] She spooked Cassandra with her description of Fanny's lively conversations with an "apothecary" Mr. Haden, but reassured her sister with a typical bit of nonsense:

> You seem to be under a mistake as to Mr H.—You call him an Apothecary; he is no Apothecary, he has never been an Apothecary, there is not an Apothecary in this Neighbourhood—the only inconvenience of the situation perhaps, but so it is—we have not a medical Man within reach—he is a Haden, nothing but a Haden, a sort of wonderful nondescript Creature on two legs, something between a Man & an Angel—but without the least spice of an Apothecary.—He is perhaps the only person not an Apothecary hereabouts.[36]

Her wit was also on display in her business dealings. Years after writing the scene from *Pride and Prejudice*, Jane

Austen encountered an officious male Lady Catherine, and she responded with the same combination of wit, honesty, and shrewd diplomacy as her heroine. While she was in London overseeing the final stages of *Emma*'s publication, her brother Henry became seriously ill. James, Edward, and Cassandra hurried to town to be with him, and when he began to mend Jane remained behind to nurse him to health. A physician who cared for Henry was a doctor to the Prince Regent, a man whom Austen "hated" because of his scandalous life and his ill treatment of his wife, and Henry let slip—as he was wont to do—that Jane was the author of several books.

Scoundrel though he was, the future George IV had some literary taste, and he and the rest of the court had been reading Austen's novels. When he learned through his physician that the author was in London, he arranged a tour of the splendid royal residence Carlton House, led by his personal librarian, the Reverend James Stanier Clarke. Clarke escorted Austen through green-walled halls, decorated with marble Ionic columns, and into the rooms with walls of crimson and blue and rose, trimmed in gold, with flowered carpets and satin hangings.[37] Jenny had little admiration for such ostentatious luxury, and less for the Prince Regent, and she must have alternated between suppressing giggles and fending off disgust.

A self-absorbed, self-deceived buffoon, the Reverend Clarke could have played Mr. Collins without having to enter into the role. He fancied himself a literary figure, and thought the little lady needed ideas for novels, so he suggested that Austen devote "some future Work [to] the Habits of Life and Character and enthusiasm of a Clergyman," one who was

"Fond of, & entirely engaged in Literature—no man's Enemy but his own."[38] He thought that it would be particularly useful to "Carry your Clergyman to Sea as the Friend of some distinguished Naval Character about a Court."[39] Clarke himself, as it turns out, had been a naval chaplain. "Write a book about me," he said in effect.

Jane delayed replying to the suggestion, and when she did she thanked Clarke for his kind comments about her book but stated she was incapable of writing the book he requested. Instead of confronting Clarke's narcissistic belief that his life was worthy of fiction, or telling him to bug off and mind his own business, she refused his suggestion with clever self-abnegation. She wrote that "the comic part of the Character I might be equal to, but not the Good, the Enthusiastic, the Literary. Such a Man's Conversation must at times be on subjects of Science and Philosophy of which I know nothing." In Austen's view, a "Classical Education, or at any rate, a very extensive acquaintance with English Literature, Ancient & Modern, appears to me quite Indispensable for the person who [would] do any justice to your Clergyman." She was quite unprepared: "I think I may boast myself to be, with all possible Vanity, the most unlearned, & uninformed Female who ever dared to be an Authoress."[40] A delicious putdown, worthy of Elizabeth Bennet's creator.

Clarke would not be dismissed so easily, and wrote back to suggest that Austen write a romance, perhaps based on the Cobourg family, which, not surprisingly, Clarke himself was serving as chaplain.[41] Austen responded with the same ironic cordiality: "You are very, very kind in your hints as to the sort of Composition which might recommend me at present." She agreed that such a historical romance "might be more to the purpose of Profit or Popularity, than such pictures of domestic life in Country Villages as I deal in." She added, "-No-[the italicizing dashes are hers], I must keep to my own style & go my own Way."[42]

Clarke never wrote again.

Austen had her private revenge. To Mary Cooke and Fanny Knight she sent a "Plan for a Novel" inspired by Clarke's suggestions. A poor but virtuous heroine finds herself "reduced to support herself and her Father by her Talents, and work for her Bread." Surrounded by villains, she is "continually cheated and defrauded of her hire, worn down to a Skeleton, and now then starved to death." Finally, she and her father escape to a humble cottage in Kamschatka where her father "finding his end approaching, throws himself on the Ground, and after 4 or 5 hours of tender advice and parental Admonition to his miserable Child, expires in a fine burst of Literary Enthusiasm, intermingled with invectives against Holder's of Tythes."[43]

When she was not making fun of Rev. Clarke, Austen was composing her next novel, *Emma*, named for its title character, the beautiful and very wealthy Emma Woodhouse. Emma lives with her doting and feeble father at Hartfield in the town of Highbury, and despite her youth she is the great lady of the town. She devotes her considerable free time to the project of improving her friend, Harriet Smith, and matching her up with the local minister, Mr. Elton. Her efforts end badly, but Emma remains oblivious to the damage she causes. The turning point comes at a picnic where she makes Miss Bates, an unstoppable chatterbox, the butt of a cruel joke. Mr. Knightley, the Woodhouses' neighbor, severely rebukes Emma for her unkindness, and Emma begins to mend. She is meanwhile giving up her unserious flirtation with the dashing but unserious Frank Churchill, and realizes that she is falling in love with Mr. Knightley, whom she finally marries.

Emma turned out to be Austen's most popular and profitable novel, and its success can be attributed partly to Clarke. While showing Jane around Carlton House, he had hinted that the Prince Regent would condescend to permit Austen to dedicate a future book to him. It would have been presumptuous for Austen to claim sufficient familiarity with the Prince Regent to dedicate a book without his permission, but since he condescended to permit the dedication, Austen had an open door. Jane's niece Caroline remembered the incident years later: "My Aunt made all proper acknowledgments at the moment, but had no intention of accepting the honor offered—until she was advised by some of her friends that she must consider the permission as a command." What was the force of royal "permission"? Jane wanted to know. "Among the many flattering attentions which I [received] from you at Carlton House," she wrote to Clarke,

> was the Information of my being at liberty to dedicate any future work to HRH the P.R. without the necessity of any Solicitation on my part. Such at least, I beleived to be your words; but as I am very anxious to be quite certain of what was intended, I intreat you to have the goodness to inform me how such a Permission is to be understood, & whether it is incumbent upon me to shew my sense of the Honour, by inscribing the Word now in the press, to H. R. H.[44]

Clarke assured her, in his inimitably unctuous manner, that she was under no obligation:

> It is certainly not *incumbent* on you to dedicate your work now in the Press to His Royal Highness: but if you wish to do the Regent that honour either now or at any future period, I am happy to send you that permission which need not require any more trouble or Solicitation on your Part.[45]

Austen concluded it was best to accept the offer, and *Emma* appeared with a dedication, composed by the publisher John Murray.

In the Austen home, "the little adventure was talked of for a while with some interest, and afforded some amusement," as we might imagine. Afterward, Caroline wrote, "my Aunt was never brought so near the precincts of the Court again— nor did she ever try to recall herself to the recollection of the Physician, Librarian or Prince, and so ended this little outburst of Royal Patronage."[46] The dedication did, however, come in handy. With Henry ill, Jane had to take on the business of publication herself, and she wrote a series of letters arranging meetings with Murray, informing the publisher that the prince had authorized a dedication, and inquiring about a delay in the printing of the book. On the last point, she told Murray that she was "disappointed & vexed by the delays of the Printers," and she wondered, "Is it likely that the Printers will be influenced to greater Dispatch & Punctuality by knowing that the Word is to be dedicated, by Permission, to the Prince Regent?"[47] Reminding the publisher of the dedication to set a fire under the printer was Henry's idea, but Jane was the one who played the card, despite her own ambivalence about the dedication itself. This ploy worked. Her letter was no sooner sent than the printer sent her page proofs for final corrections.[48] In another time, Jane might have become a CEO of a publishing house.

By later standards, Austen never achieved literary celebrity during her lifetime. Her books sold well, and she earned what to her was a considerable sum of money from them (*Emma* alone brought in 450 pounds);[49] but by the end of the century a literary celebrity like Dickens was selling hundreds of thousands of copies of his serialized novels, and getting rich. The difference is due partly to the standards of her time. The age of literary advertising and literary marketing was only beginning, and no authors of the early nineteenth century sold books at the rate of a Dickens. Even within her world, however, Austen was less than a literary sensation. It is ironic that *Emma*, finished in March 1814 and published in December of the following year, should bring Austen closest to literary celebrity, for she feared that that book would be panned by people who liked her earlier work. She wondered if anyone would enjoy Emma herself, and realized that the book was even lighter in tone than *Pride and Prejudice*:

> My greatest anxiety at present is that this 4th work [should] not disgrace what was good in the others. But on this point I will do myself the justice to declare that whatever may be my wishes for its' success, I am very strongly haunted by the idea that to those Readers who have preferred P&P, it will appear inferior in Wit, & to those who have preferred MP. very inferior in good Sense.[50]

She joked to Cassandra that her books decreased in sense in inverse proportion to the price the publisher paid for them. *Emma*, she theorized, must be her "stupidest" book, because it was the most profitable. And joking or not, it would have irked Austen to no end to have people think she was sacrificing good sense and good writing for profit. In her novels, she concerned herself more with reality of situation and honesty of character than any sort of fantastical romanticizing. She wanted to portray the world as it really is.

A GREAT OBSERVER

Jesus told His disciples to become like children. This has often been understood, sentimentally, as an encouragement to naivete, as if Jesus wanted His disciples to go through life with eyes wide in undiscerning simplicity: To be a child is to be a beautiful soul, quavering timidly before a hard and indifferent world. This is precisely the opposite of what Jesus intended. A child's ability to see through cant and pretense is proverbial, and this native shrewdness is what Jesus is after. Adults take pretense far too seriously. To "become as a child" means to not take the world as seriously as it takes itself. Jesus knew that it takes a child to notice that the emperor has no clothes. Children see through pretense because they know how to pretend.

Jenny Austen was, as Brutus says of Cassius, "a great observer of men," and she saw through pretense and folly because even as a writer she remained Jenny Austen. As every critic notices, her novels are full of shrewdly observed characters, but Austen had equal insight into the people around her.

She noticed what they wore, how they spoke, what they said, and how they responded to others, and she saw the connections between these different facets of character. Her descriptions of folly are most vivid. One man is "a little sillier than the Colonel,"[51] and she saw quite through pretension: "They live in a handsome style and are rich, and she seemed to like to be rich, and we gave her to understand that we were far from being so; she will soon feel therefore that we are not worth her acquaintance."[52] She was suspicious of people who lacked discernment. When she met one Mrs. Armstrong, she took a walk with her "on the Cobb," a portion of Bath: "She seems to like people rather too easily—she thought the Downes pleasant &c &c."[53]

Anna's sudden engagement to Ben Lefroy caught Austen and her family by surprise, though, keen observer that she was, Austen noted that "there was *that* about her which kept us in a constant preparation for something." She considered Ben "sensible, certainly very religious, well connected & with some Independence," but she worried that "there is an unfortunate dissimilarity of Taste between them" in that "he hates company & she is very fond of it." That disparity, the "queerness of Temper on his side & much unsteadiness on hers, is untoward."[54] The next month, in October 1813, Ben was offered a "highly eligible" curacy in the Church of England, pending ordination. Ben was uncertain about "taking orders so early." Faced with the choice of taking the curacy and having Anna or refusing the curacy and losing her, he said he would "give Anna up rather than do what he does not approve."[55] Austen did not dislike Ben Lefroy. She joked that she suspected Ben was secretly in love with *her* rather than with her niece: "I rather imagine indeed that Neices are seldom chosen but in compliment to some Aunt or other," she wrote to Anna in September 1814. "I dare say Ben was in love with me once & [would] never have thought of *you* if he had not supposed me dead of a Scarlet fever."[56] Still, she found his attitude "maddish." Though Ben and Anna were continuing the engagement, Austen was convinced "it cannot last."[57] It did. Ben married Anna in November 1814, he was ordained in 1817, and the marriage produced seven children before Ben died in 1829.

Though Austen's prediction proved wrong, it is instructive to see her mind at work evaluating Ben and Anna's character and situation. She evaluated Ben not only on the basis of his personal characteristics ("sensible," "very religious"), but also on his situation in life (e.g., "well connected"). For Austen, a person is not only what he or she is in the privacy of his individuality; a person *is* his social role. Her assessment of their relationship was not, moreover, a sum of their individual traits, but more an analysis of a chemical reaction. Their prospects depended as much on their differences and similarities, on the strange alchemy of the two together, as on anything each had in him- or herself.

While Austen was enduring the symptoms of what turned out to be her final illness, her niece Fanny began to write letters full of amusing whimsy that raised Jane's spirits considerably. She wrote back with an insightful character sketch of her niece. "You are inimitable, irresistable," Aunt Jane said: "You are so odd!—& all the time, so perfectly natural—so peculiar in yourself, & yet so like everybody else." Jane found in Fanny a unique combination of sense and fancy[58] "the most astonishing part of your Character is, that with so much Imagination, so much flight of Mind, such unbounded Fancies, you should have such excellent Judgment in what you do!" Jane attributed this remarkable combination to "Religious Principle."[59] She rebuked Fanny for forcing a suitor, James Wildman, to read some of Aunt Jane's novels: "my strongest sensation of all is astonishment at your being able to press him on the subject so perseveringly." Her behavior provoked this description: "You are the oddest Creature!——Nervous enough in some respects, but in others perfectly without nerves. Quite unrepulsible, hardened and impudent."[60] There is playful irony here, but there is also the shrewd insight of a child who enjoys watching people wear masks but also knows there are faces on the other side.

This love for and fascination with people as they really are could not help but spill into her novels, but perhaps the most remarkable aspect of her characterization is that she recognized and rendered the basic humanity of them all. She depicted villains and heroes, catty backstabbers and retiring bookworms, pompous clerics and charitable aristocrats, but none is one-dimensional. A few of Austen's characters are more like traditional villains. Fanny Price's Aunt Norris is bullying and aggressive, and Mrs. John Dashwood in *Sense and Sensibility* approaches caricature in her tight-minded greediness. Lady Catherine de Bourgh threatens to become caricature as well, but even in these cases, Austen created complex characters who have understandable, if petty, motivations. E. M. Forster noted,

Why do the characters in Jane Austen give us a slightly new pleasure each time they come in, as opposed to the merely repetitive pleasure that is caused by a character in Dickens? . . . The answer to this question can be put in several ways; that, unlike Dickens, she was a real artist, that she never stooped to caricature, etc. But the best reply is that her characters, though smaller than his, are more highly organized. They function all round, and even if her plot made greater demands on them than it does they would still be adequate. . . . . All the Jane Austen characters are ready for an extended life which the scheme of her books seldom requires them to lead, and that is why they lead their actual lives so satisfactorily.[61]

Austen never forgot that her villains and villainesses are also humans. Her breadth of her sympathy is a rare commodity among novelists. We are meant to laugh at Mr. Collins, the pompously obsequious cleric in *Pride and Prejudice*, but we laugh at him with human sympathy. We know Collins is a buffoon, but few readers hate him. Mrs. Elton, the Bath wife whom another clergyman, Mr. Elton, brings back to live at the Highbury of Emma Woodhouse, is all-knowing and all-controlling. Nothing Emma can do or say, nothing that Highbury can offer comes close to the wonders of Maple Grove. Yet, annoying as she is, Mrs. Elton is not demonized or caricatured.

Austen wanted her novels to be a training ground in moral discernment, and to train her readers well she needed to avoid the reassuring clarities of Gothic romance and melodrama. She wanted readers to distrust the smooth French manners of Henry Crawford in *Mansfield Park*, but she made him so winning and attractive that readers hardly know whether he is going to turn out to be a transformed lover or an unreformed cad. Mary Crawford, Henry's worldly and seductive sister, is an even more impressive, and risky, creation, a villainess who, like Milton's Satan, leaves a far more powerful impression than the book's heroine. The British philosopher Gilbert Ryle got Austen wrong on many points, but he got this part mostly right: "Except for cardboard characters like William Elliot, Mrs. Clay, and Willoughby's wife, Jane Austen dispenses with the sacred Siamese-cows, Reason-Passion, Virtue-Vice, Spirit-Flesh, Saint-Sinner, Salvation-Damnation, etc. People differ in all shades and hues of all colors. No one is just White or just Black."[62]

Austen's work was beginning to be noticed, not only by the Prince Regent. *Emma* brought Austen recognition from a more discerning quarter when, in March 1816, the *Quarterly Review* devoted an article to her work, written by Walter Scott. Austen had risen to literary heights that few achieve. To be noticed with approval by the giant of the literary world was no small achievement. This all happened in the spring of 1816.

Austen did not live to enjoy her moment of modest celebrity for long. A year later, she was mortally ill, and by July 1817 she was dead.

6

DEATH

Austen was, as she would have said, "stout" throughout her life. She had trouble seeing, and suffered colds and other ailments, but she was not one to complain about her own health. When she found herself getting "near complaint" in her final year, she reminded herself that it was all ordained by God.[1]

But during 1816–1817, her health collapsed. It was only one of the collapses of that year. Henry's bank failed, putting the family, especially the women, at financial risk, and leaving Henry permanently deflated with the memory of disappointing so many who had trusted him. A ship Charles commanded wrecked, and though Charles was exonerated, he was anxious about getting future commissions. A Chawton family, the Hintons, brought a lawsuit against Edward. He eventually cut down a large section of one of his forests to raise money to pay them off, but the suit left his possession on his Hampshire properties—including Chawton—uncertain for some time. When James Leigh-Perrot died, leaving his entire fortune to his wife,

Jane could not conceal her disappointment: "I am ashamed to say that the shock of my Uncle's Will brought on a relapse," she confided to Charles in what proved her last letter to her little brother, "& I was so ill on Friday & thought myself so likely to be worse." Mrs. Austen "has borne the forgetfulness of her extremely well;—her expectations for herself were never beyond the extreme of moderation, & she thinks with you that my Uncle always looked forward to surviving her."[2]

Jane was suffering too. As early as the spring of 1816, she began showing symptoms of what would later be known as Addison's disease. Identified by Dr. Thomas Addison in 1849, Addison's disease is a disorder in the endocrine system that causes fatigue, muscle weakness, joint pains, and darkening of the skin. Austen suffered back pains, and spent more of her time in a makeshift sofa constructed from two chairs in the sitting room at Chawton Cottage. She refused the real sofa because her mother, also ailing, needed it, and she knew that her mother would yield it to her if she found out that Jane was more comfortable there. To her last days, she maintained the pretense that she preferred the chairs to the sofa.

Yet, her illness dampened neither her comic spirits nor her creativity. Fanny Knight wrote to her frequently, and Jane was delighted by a niece whose humor and style so resembled her own. "As to making an adequate return for such a Letter as yours my dearest Fanny," she wrote in the spring of 1817, "it is absolutely impossible; if I were to labour at it all the rest of my Life & live to the age of Methusalah, I could never accomplish anything too long & so perfect."[3] She continued to look at the world with bemusement. "We saw numberless postchaises full of Boys pass by yesterday morning," she wrote to her nephew James Edward Austen Leigh:

> Full of future heroes, legislators, fools and villains. You have never thanked me for my last letter which went by the Cheese. I cannot bear not to be thanks. You will not pay us a visit yet of course, we must not think of it. Your Mother must get well first, and you must go to Oxford and not be elected; after that, a little change of scene may be good for you, and your physicians I hope will order you to the sea, or to a house by the side of a very considerable pond.[4]

Chawton Cottage, of course, was the site of a "very considerable pond."

She was still writing for publication as well. Henry arranged for the return of the manuscript of *Susan* (*Northanger Abbey*), and Jane began revising it for future publication. Between the sale of the manuscript and her re-acquisition, another novel named *Susan* had been published, and so Austen rewrote the whole, giving the name Catherine Morland to her heroine. By August 1816 she had finished her last complete novel, published as *Persuasion* the following autumn. She was still laboring to perfect her writing. The first ending of *Persuasion* failed to satisfy, and she revised it into one of the most famous endings in English literature. She found the original ending "tame and flat." In the revised ending, Captain Wentworth overhears a conversation between Anne Elliot and Captain Harville where they compare the faithfulness and fickleness of men and women. Stung by Anne's opinions, Wentworth writes a note declaring that he loved her always. Early in 1817, Jane began *Sanditon*, but within a few months she was too exhausted to continue. What we have of *Sanditon* shows that she had lost none of her literary powers, but she laid it aside and never returned to her novels after March 1817.

By May, her symptoms had gotten worse, and her family moved her to Winchester to come under the care of the respected Dr. Lyford. Jane and Cassandra lived on College Street, close to the Winchester School and the cathedral where she was later buried. Cassandra cared for her day and night, Henry and James visited to administer the sacrament, and Edward was regularly at her side. Her life was ending as it began, surrounded by her brothers and her best friend, Cassandra. Henry recalled that during her last months she endured "all the varying pain, irksomeness, and tedium, attendant on decaying nature, with more than resignation—with a truly elastic cheerfulness. She retained her faculties, her memory, her fancy, her temper, her affections, warm, clear, and unimpaired, to the last."[5]

Nieces visited too. Accompanied by Anna, Caroline paid her last visit to Chawton in January 1817:

> She was keeping her room but said she would see us, and we went up to her—She was in her dressing gown and was sitting quite like an invalid in an arm chair—but she got up, and kindly greeted us—and then pointing to seats which had been arranged for us by the fire, she said, "There's a chair for the married lady, and a little stool for *you*, Caroline."—It is strange, but those trifling words are the last of her's that I can remember—for I retain *no* recollection *at* all of what was said

by any one in the conversation that of course ensued. . . . I was struck by the alteration in herself—She was very pale—her voice was weak and low and there was about her, a general appearance of debility and suffering; but I have been told that she never *had* much actual pain. . . . She was not equal to the exertion of talking to us, and our visit to the sick room was a very short one—Aunt Cassandra soon taking us away—I don't suppose we stayed a quarter of an hour; and *I* never saw Aunt Jane again.[6]

Like Henry, Caroline and Anna found that Austen's personality had changed little: "Her sweetness of temper never failed her; she was considerate and grateful to those who attended on her, and at times, when feeling rather better, her playfulness of spirit prevailed, and she amused them even in their sadness."[7]

The last weeks were a wrenching series of improvements and declines. Charles captured the emotional upheavals in his diary:

Thursday 12th June: Received a letter from Henry acquainting me with Dear Jane's illness took a place in the mail for Winchester. *Friday 13th June*: Arrived at Winchester at 5 in the morning found my Sister very ill. *Saturday 14th June*: Henry went to Chawton. Jane continuing very ill. *Sunday 15th June*: Went to morning service at the Cathedral. Jane a shade better. *Monday 16th June*: Rode to Chawton on Henrys Horse arrived at dinner & found my Mother very poorly. *Wednesday 18th June*: I returned to Winchester on top of the Coach, found Dear Jane rather better. *Thursday 19th June*:

Jane a little better. Saw her twice & in the evening for the last time in the world as I greatly fear, the Doctor having no hope of her final recovery.[8]

Fanny's diary shows the same variation from "bad account of Aunt Jane Austen from Uncle Henry" on June 12 to a "better account of dear Aunt Jane" on the seventeenth.[9] Mrs. Austen reported to Anna on June 19 that "Jane has had a better Night than she has had for many weeks, and has been comfortable all day, Mr Lyford says he thinks better of her than he has ever done."[10] By the middle of June, despite slight revivals, the family was preparing itself for the worst.

Jane knew what was coming too. As early as April 27, she had drawn up a will, bequeathing everything she owned to Cassandra and naming her executrix, but leaving a legacy of 50£ to Henry and the same to Madame Bigeon, Henry's housekeeper.[11] After she died, Cassandra sent a lock of her sister's hair to Anne Sharp, tutor to the Knight children of Godmersham, whom Jane had befriended over years of visits in Kent.[12]

None of the main characters in Austen's novels die. Few people are injured or seriously threatened. Austen, of course, knew death. Her mother survived her by many years, but her father died when she was thirty. Throughout her life, her family was touched by death—the death of Mrs. Austen's sister Jane Cooper, the death of Tom Fowle, the death of James's first wife and Edward's wife, the death of Aunt Philadelphia and cousin Eliza, the death of Madam Lefroy. Austen did not live in a deathless bubble. She was acquainted with grief, but nothing displays Austen's playfulness and piety—her playful piety—so clearly as her attitude toward death. In the face of death, she remained Jenny Austen.

She expressed her sympathy and regret for friends who lost loved ones, and her hope that God will comfort and restore the living. She often focused on the comfort brought by an easy death: "Poor woman!" she said of one dying friend. "May her end be peaceful & easy, as the Exit we have witnessed!"[13] When Edward's wife died, she found it "consolatory to reflect on the shortness of the sufferings which led her from this World to a better."[14] Elizabeth Leigh's death brought sorrow, but she added, "[T]he death of a person at her advanced age, so fit to die, & by her own feelings so *ready* to die, is not to be regretted."[15]

On the other hand, Austen had an impudent attitude toward death that sometimes bordered on childish flippancy. Her *Juvenalia* are full of violent deaths, played for laughs. In *Love and Freindship*, Edward dies after a carriage accident with a pun on his lips: "Laura I fear I have been overturned." When the real-life "Mrs. Hall of Sherbourn was brought to bed yesterday of a dead child, some weeks before she expected, oweing to a fright," Austen speculated snarkily, "I suppose she happened unawares to look at her husband."[16] When a Bath acquaintance, Marianne Mapleton died young, Austen reacted cynically to the family's grief and overwrought praise of their dead daughter and sister: "So affectionate a family must suffer severely; & many a girl on early death has been praised into an Angel I believe, on slighter pretensions to Beauty, Sense & Merit than Marianne."[17] Miss Holder was "very fond of talking of her deceased brother & Sister, whose memories she cherishes with an Enthusiasm which tho perhaps a little affected, is not unpleasing."[18] When Jane read a newspaper report concerning the battle of Alameida, she wrote, "How horrible it is to have so many people killed!—And what a blessing that one cares for none of them!"[19] When she saw the elderly minister Dr. Hall in a carriage, she commented that he was "in such very deep mourning that either his mother, his wife, or himself must be dead." She showed a creepy interest in the appearance of corpses: "I suppose you see the Corpse," she wrote Cassandra about Elizabeth Knight's body. "How does it appear?"[20]

Her Christian faith had always come to most explicit expression at the margins of life, where death and destruction threatened. When she learned that her cousin, Philadelphia Walter, had lost her father, Jane wrote to express her sympathy: "the Goodness which made him valuable on Earth, will make him Blessed in Heaven."[21] When her brother Edward's wife, Elizabeth Knight, died, Jane took comfort in the fact that Edward "has a religious Mind to bear him up, & a Disposition that will gradually lead him to comfort." To Cassandra, who was visiting Godmersham at the time, she added, "May the Almighty sustain you all."[22] When Sir John Moore died uttering final words more patriotic than religious, Jane wished that "Sir John had united something of the Christian with the Hero in his death."[23] This is especially revealing because Moore's last words captured so perfectly the intense patriotism that gripped England during the years of war with France. Austen recognized the difference between love of country and Christian faith, and thought death the time for faith rather than patriotism.[24] While visiting London in the fall of 1814, she had a chance to see Benjamin West's painting *Christ's Rejection by the*

Elders. She found it gratifying, "indeed the first representation of our Saviour which ever at all contented me."[25]

She faced her own approaching death in the same spirit. Writing to her friend Anne Sharp, she praised her brothers' and Cassandra's efforts to make her comfortable: "Every dear Brother so affectionate & so anxious!—And as for my Sister!—Words must fail me in any attempt to describe what a Nurse she has been to me." She was happy to be feeling better, glad that "the Providence of God has restored me," and she hoped for improvement before death: "may I be more fit to appear before him when I *am* summoned, than I [should] have been now."[26] In her last surviving letter, to Francis Tilson, she commended Cassandra's nursing: "my dearest sister, my tender, watchful, indefatigable nurse . . . As to what I owe to her, and to the anxious affection of all my beloved family on this occasion, I can only cry over it, and pray to God to bless them more and more." She gave details of her illness, but brought herself up short: "I am getting to near complaint. It has been the appointment of God, however secondary causes may have operated."[27]

Years before, after recovering from a serious illness, Mrs. Austen had written a poem entitled "Dialogue between Death & Mrs. Austen," which ended with the "old fellow" Death being chased away by the prayers of George Austen and the care of the Austen daughters. Jane did not win her dialogue with death, but her mind turned to comic poetry in the last days of her life. On June 15, St. Swithin's Day, it rained heavily on the horse racing at Worthy Down near Winchester, and Jane, surmising that it must be the Saint's revenge, dictated a light-hearted poem, her last composition.[28]

When Winchester races first took their beginning
It is said the good people forgot their old Saint
Not applying at all for the leave of Saint Swithin
And that William of Wykeham's approval was faint.
The races however were fixed and determined
The company came and the Weather was charming
The Lords and the Ladies were satine'd and ermined
And nobody saw any future alarming.—
But when the old Saint was informed of these doings
He made but one Spring from his Shrine to the Roof
Of the Palace which now lies so sadly in ruins
And then he addressed them all standing aloof.
'Oh! subjects rebellious! Oh Venta depraved
When once we are buried you think we are gone
But behold me immortal! By vice you're enslaved
You have sinned and must suffer, ten farther he said
These races and revels and dissolute measures
With which you're debasing a neighboring Plain
Let them stand—You shall meet with your curse in your pleasures
Set off for your course, I'll pursue with my rain.
Ye cannot but know my command o'er July
Henceforward I'll triumph in shewing my powers
Shift your race as you will it shall never be dry
The curse upon Venta is July in showers—'.[29]

It is entirely appropriate that her last piece of writing should be comic verse, and that it should deal merrily with a religious theme. Jenny Austen to the last.

On July 17, Cassandra went to town on an errand, and

she returned to find her sister recovering from a faint. Jane was "able to give me a minute account of her seizure & when the clock struck 6 she was talking quietly to me. I cannot say how soon afterwards she was seized again with the same faintness . . . She felt herself to be dying about half an hour before she became tranquil and apparently unconscious."[30] Cassandra wrote, "During that half hour was her struggle, poor Soul! she said she could not tell us what she suffered, tho she complained of little fixed pain. When I asked her if there was any thing she wanted, her answer was she wanted nothing but death & some of her words were 'God grant me patience, Pray for me Oh Pray for me.'"[31]

They were Jane's last words. The next day, July 18, 1817, she died at age forty-one.

Only a few family members attended the funeral. Henry made the arrangements, and Frank and Edward came to pay their respects. James was unable to attend, and sent James Edward in his place. Before they closed the coffin, Cassandra took some locks of hair as a keepsake.[32] Jane was buried in the Winchester Cathedral, her gravestone bearing an inscription written by Henry:

In memory of
JANE AUSTEN,
youngest daughter of the late
Revd. GEORGE AUSTEN,
formerly Rector of Steventon in this County.
She departed this Life on the 18th July 1817,
aged 41, after a long illness supported with

the patience and the hopes of a Christian.

The benevolence of her heart,

the sweetness of her temper, and

the extraordinary endowments of her mind

obtained the regard of all who knew her, and

the warmest love of her intimate connections.

Their grief is in proportion to their affection

they know their loss to be irreparable,

but in the deepest affliction they are consoled

by a firm though humble hope that her charity,

devotion, faith and purity have rendered

her soul acceptable in the sight of her

REDEEMER.

For a long time after, Anna Lefroy continued the habit of storing away things to tell Jane: "I miss her; it had become so much a habit with me to put by things in my mind with a reference to her and to say to myself, 'I shall keep this for Aunt Jane.'"[33]

FROM DIVINE JANE
BACK TO JENNY

ane was so fearful about the risks of publishing *Sense and Sensibility* that she put aside a little of her meager funds to pay the publisher if the book failed. She need not have worried. Published in 1811, the print run of a thousand copies sold out by the summer of 1813. Released into the wide world, Jenny's first book was able to make its own way. Sixteen-year-old Princess Charlotte reacted viscerally, if ungrammatically: "Maryanne & me are very alike in disposition, that certainly I am not so good, the same imprudence, &c however remain very like."[1] By the time *Sense and Sensibility* sold out, *Pride and Prejudice* had already been in circulation for nearly a year, selling well. Jane's books were popular among men as well as women.

Critics did not quite know what to do with Jenny Austen. They were used to sensational Gothic romances or passionate novels of sensibility. They were also used to sniffily dismissing novels as intellectually fluffy, if not morally dangerous, and found value only in those few novels that could plausibly be seen to offer overt moral lessons. Confronted with the realism, plausibility, irony, and understated morality of *Sense and Sensibility* and *Pride and Prejudice*, reviewers paid their respects, but with more than a little puzzlement about what they were reading. They knew it was different, but could not quite tell how.

One can hardly blame them. Austen had invented a new genre—the modern novel—and it was a genre no one had yet learned to read. All English novelists since Austen have had to work within, or renounce, the genre she made her own. All English novelists since Austen are Jenny's children.

In themselves, the reviews were respectful enough. A "very pleasing and entertaining" work said one of *Sense and Sensibility*, and another added that it was "well written; the characters are in genteel life, naturally drawn and judiciously supported. The incidents are probable, and highly pleasing, and interesting; the conclusion such as the reader must wish it should be."[2] They might have been grading a junior high essay. *Pride and Prejudice* was greeted with somewhat more enthusiasm. Poet and playwright Richard Brinsley Sheridan pronounced *Pride and Prejudice* as "one of the cleverest things" he had ever read, and Henry delighted Jane with the report that a literary maven had concluded that the book was far too clever to have been written by a woman.[3]

Emma brought Austen's reputation to its highest point during her lifetime, along with a reviewer who understood what Austen was up to. Sir Walter Scott was as perceptive about Austen's talents as the Prince Regent's librarian James Stanier Clarke was imbecilic. Scott recognized that her talents were quite different from, and, in her field, superior to his own:

> That young lady has a talent for describing the involvements
> and feelings and characters of ordinary life, which is to me
> the most wonderful I ever met with. The big Bow-Wow strain
> I can do myself like any now going; but the exquisite touch
> which renders ordinary common-place things and characters
> interesting from the truth of the description and the senti-
> ment is denied to me.[4]

Jane's publisher, John Murray, sent a copy of the review, for which she was grateful, but she stiffly commented: "The Authoress of *Emma* has no reason I think to complain of her treatment in it—except in the total omission of *Mansfield Park*.—I cannot but be sorry that so clever a Man as the Reviewer of *Emma*, should consider it as unworthy of being noticed."[5]

Several years after Austen's death, Richard Whately published a perceptive review of her work in the *Quarterly Review* that set the terms for much of later Austen criticism. For the first time, Austen was set alongside the greatest writers of the Western tradition, Homer and Shakespeare. Whately recognized that Austen aimed to instruct, but that she instructed obliquely rather than directly. Her novels were better than those of Evangelicals like Hannah Moore and Maria Edgewood, he argued, since they tended to put their "avowedly didactic purpose" ahead of probability. Austen left the reader to "collect" moral lessons from the narrative, and Whately found her method more effective.[6]

But the times were changing. A different sensibility—passionate, romantic, Gothic, everything that Austen found so amusingly improbable—was taking form in the Romantic movement. Austen's books went out of print for a time, and when in print did not sell particularly well. Charlotte Brontë was amazed that Henry Lewes found Austen's books so appealing, writing in bewilderment in 1848:

> Why do you like Miss Austen so very much? I am puzzled on that point. . . . I had not seen *Pride and Prejudice* till I had read that sentence of yours, and then I got the book. And what did I find? An accurate daguerrotyped portrait of a commonplace face; a carefully fenced, highly cultivated garden, with neat borders and delicate flowers; but no glance of a bright vivid physiognomy, no open country, no fresh air, no blue hill, no bonny beck. I should hardly like to live with her ladies and gentlemen, in their elegant but confined houses. These observations will probably irritate you. but I shall run the risk.[7]

Obsession with George Sand she understood, but where Sand is "sagacious and profound; Miss Austen is only shrewd and observant." A week later, Brontë wrote again: "Miss Austen being, as you say, without 'sentiment,' without poetry, maybe is sensible (more real than true), but she cannot be great."[8] Brontë was moderate compared to Mark Twain, who professed a desire to exhume Austen and beat her skull with her shinbone whenever he tried to read one of her novels. When Austen's nephew James Edward wrote his memoir in 1870, he commented that "seldom has any literary reputation been of such slow growth as that of Jane Austen."[9]

James Edward's work reawakened interest in Austen , and after mid-century, times were changing again. The great historian, poet, and politician Thomas Babington Macaulay described Austen as second only to Shakespeare as a "truthful drawer of character,"[10] Oxford's A. C. Bradley delivered a lecture that marked the beginning of serious critical attention to Austen, and by the beginning of the twentieth century Henry James could see a commercialized cult of Austen in the making. There was, he noted, a "body of publishers, editors, illustrator, producers of the pleasant twaddle of magazines" who discovered "their 'dear,' our dear, everybody's dear Jane so infinitely to their material purpose."[11] But the Victorians created an imaginary Austen. The best critics recognized her moral concerns and praised her as a stylist,[12] but many responded to a sanitized and civilized Austen—an Austen sanitized because she had been bowdlerized, an Austen who could never even deign to notice bad breath, much less complain about it to her sister. James Edward bears significant responsibility for this perception. Even her physical appearance was adjusted to Victorian sensibilities. The twisted miniature painted by her sister was softened into Victorian smoothness for James Edward's memoir.

Literary critic Roger Sales has argued that the family embarked on a re-invention of Austen soon after her death, blunting the satiric strain of her novels and turning her into a quaintly domestic figure. He makes his case persuasively by comparing the edited letters that James Edward included in his memoir with the full text. In one letter, James leaves out "a level-headed description of financial transactions; the hope that somebody would not be 'cruel enough to consent' . . . to an invitation to dinner and an inquiry as to whether Cassandra has had time to discover whether there is anybody who is more boring than a certain Sarah Mitchell." Austen's letter closes with "Give my love to little Cassandra! I hope she found my Bed comfortable last night and has not filled it with fleas." Austen's nephew obligingly left out the part about the fleas, one of the best bits in the letter.

Another of James's letters leaves out "Austen complaining to a tradesman about the quality of some currant bushes that had been purchased earlier; the fact that it was Henry rather than she who was fatigued by the journey; and some confidently given advice for one of her other brothers on the best roads to travel when coming to London." With these omissions, her nephew "denies her strength, both of purpose and of physique, as well as not allowing her knowledge of the world beyond home." James left off the end of this letter too, which makes reference to the previously mentioned elegant "naked Cupids over the Mantlepiece" in the drawing room at a London school, and Austen's observation that these "must be a fine study for Girls," in the absence of which "one should never have Smelt Instruction." Apparently, he could not bear the thought of his dear aunt contemplating naked cupids. Purged of cultural or political interest, cleansed of the social edginess of Austen's heroines, stripped of her punchy humor, the Victorian Austen was transfigured, bizarrely, into a celebrant of home and hearth, of feminine decorum and private domesticity. Much as he admired Austen, the novelist Anthony Trollope was no help. Somehow, he found in Austen a set of lessons in good housekeeping: "Throughout all her works, and they are not many, a sweet lesson of homely household womanly virtue is ever being taught"—which can only mean he didn't read the novels with much attention.

In *The Civilizing Process*, Norbert Elias investigates how the "modes of behaviour considered typical of people who are civilized in a Western way" came about.[13] Through a careful survey of etiquette books and other documents dealing with topics like table manners, blowing one's nose, spitting, the deportment of the body, facial expressions, and the control of bodily functions, Elias argues that Westerners went through a gradual and uneven affective transformation during the sixteenth and seventeenth centuries. By the end of the process, behaviors considered normal in the Middle Ages had been ruled "barbarous," and the civilized separation from barbarity signaled major changes in feelings of delicacy, shame, refinement, and repugnance. During the centuries following Shakespeare's death, the performances of his work were "civilized." Though Austen was never bawdy in public as Shakespeare was, she was sharp and satiric. The Austen revival of the nineteenth century didn't allow Austen to be Austen. The Victorian era revived a "civilized" Austen.

JENNY RECOVERED

It was not until the twentieth century that Jenny reemerged from behind the fictitious flowsy Jane Austen that had been concocted by her family and their Victorian collaborators. Only in the twentieth century did critics and readers recover a sense of the impish satiric laughter that is Austen's characteristic tone. Austen invented the modern novel, and the recovery of the full Austen occurred with the rise of modernist fiction.

Rudyard Kipling recovered Jane as a writer for men. In

what C. S. Lewis called Kipling's worst story, the 1924 "The Janeites," Kipling puts Austen in the trenches, where British soldiers have found consolation in Austen's novels while enduring the terrors of trench warfare. They even formed a secret society of Janeites. For some, Austen awakens a distant memory of happier days at home. One character, in Kipling's trademark dialect, says,

> You've got to be a Janeite in your 'eart, or you won't have any success. An' yet he made me a Janeite! I read all her six books now for pleasure 'tween times in the shop; an' it brings it all back—down to the smell of the glue-paint on the screens. You take it from me, Brethren, there's no one to touch Jane when you're in a tight place. Gawd bless 'er, whoever she was.

Others find that Jane provides a ready-made classification system for the characters they encounter:

> There was a hospital-train fillin' up, an' one of the Sisters—a grey-headed one—ran at me wavin' 'er red 'ands an' sayin' there wasn't room for a louse in it. I was past carin'. But she went on talkin' and talkin' about the war, an' her pa in Ladbroke Grove, an' 'ow strange for 'er at 'er time of life to be doin' this work with a lot o' men, an' next war, 'ow the nurses 'ud 'ave to wear khaki breeches on account o' the mud, like the Land Girls; an' that reminded 'er, she'd boil me an egg if she could lay 'ands on one, for she'd run a chicken-farm once. You never 'eard anythin' like it—outside o' Jane. It set me off laughin' again. Then a woman with a nose an'

teeth on 'er, marched up. "What's all this?" she says. "What do you want?" "Nothing," I says, "only make Miss Bates, there, stop talkin' or I'll die." "Miss Bates?" she says. "What in 'Eaven's name makes you call 'er that?" "Because she is," I says. "D'you know what you're sayin'?" she says, an' slings her bony arm round me to get me off the ground. "'Course I do," I says, "an' if you knew Jane you'd know too."[14]

It was Virginia Woolf, however, who recaptured the original feel of Austen's work. Importantly, she turned to the *Juvenalia* and found a highly sophisticated, laughing fifteen-year-old writing for an audience bigger than her schoolroom. Woolf looked past the legend and found Jenny, and in finding Jenny she found Jane:

Girls of fifteen are always laughing. They laugh when Mr. Binney helps himself to salt instead of sugar. They almost die of laughing when old Mrs. Tomkins sits down upon the cat. But they are crying the moment after. They have no fixed abode from which they see that there is something eternally laughable in human nature, some quality in men and women that for ever excites our satire. They do not know that Lady Greville who snubs, and poor Maria who is snubbed, are permanent features of every ballroom. But Jane Austen knew it from her birth upwards. One of those fairies who perch upon cradles must have taken her a flight through the world directly she was born. When she was laid in the cradle again she knew not only what the world looked like, but had already chosen her kingdom. She had agreed that if she might rule over that territory, she would covet no other. Thus at fifteen she had few illusions about other people and none about herself.

Woolf perceived that Jane's concentration on the commonplace was not a want of imagination, but an excess. As much as Wordsworth, she was capable of seeing a world in a grain of sand, of opening a momentary encounter into a world:

> In The Watsons she gives us a foretaste of this power; she makes us wonder why an ordinary act of kindness, as she describes it, becomes so full of meaning. In her masterpieces, the same gift is brought to perfection. Here is nothing out of the way; it is midday in Northamptonshire; a dull young man is talking to rather a weakly young woman on the stairs as they go up to dress for dinner, with housemaids passing. But, from triviality, from commonplace, their words become suddenly full of meaning, and the moment for both one of the most memorable in their lives. It fills itself; it shines; it glows; it hangs before us, deep, trembling, serene for a second; next, the housemaid passes, and this drop, in which all the happiness of life has collected, gently subsides again to become part of the ebb and flow of ordinary existence.

Woolf lamented that Austen died at the height of her powers, speculating that Austen might have ventured beyond her chosen limitations had she lived, and would have become a precursor to Henry James and Marcel Proust.[15]

Over the last half century, critics have increasingly tried to see Austen in the context of her surrounding culture; and they realize just how much she knew about eighteenth-century English society and how often she seems to be commenting on those things. Beyond the critics, Austen is taken seriously by philosophers, ethicists, and even theologians. Gilbert Ryle found similarities between Austen's outlook and the writings of philosophical contemporaries like Shaftesbury, Mandeville, Adam Smith, and Frances Hutcheson, and Alasdair MacIntyre includes a section on Austen's ethics in his epochal book *After Virtue*. Since the middle of the twentieth century, scholars have recognized Austen not only as a superior novelist but as an important thinker.

The real Austen, however, remains to be recovered in the popular imagination, and the recovery requires, among other things, a recovery of a more accurate conception of the artistic life. Since the Romantic period, artists have been known for their pompous self-promotion. Every poet is a dashingly brilliant Byronic headline grabber. Every painter is a Picasso, bedding his models during the free moments of the day. Every writer is a Hemingway who embarks on safaris between books, or a sexually ambiguous Iris Murdoch, or a Sylvia Plath fluttering on the edges of sanity. Since the Romantic era, many artists have invested as much effort into forming themselves into works of art as they have to their art itself. Real artists are outliers, broodingly rejecting or raucously celebrating the world. The fact that most artists and writers do not look anything like this picture does not matter. They are merely artisans, not *artistes*.

Humility is the last virtue we associate with an artist, but contrary to post-Romantic mythology, art demands humility. Only a humble sculptor will submit himself to the shape and contours of a particular rock. Only the humble painter is willing to conform to the play of color and shape, and to bow before the qualities of the paint itself. Only a humble composer acknowledges and works within the givens of sound, and only a humble writer submits to the demands of her material. Austen was such a writer. She recognized her own smallness, and she achieved artistic greatness because she recognized her limitations and joyfully worked within them, because she refused to outgrow being Jenny.

Dante wrote out of frustrated love and a conviction of his prophetic inspiration. Shakespeare wrote to give something to his actors to perform, and for the money. Dickens wrote to redress his shame at his failed father and to express his anger at a world that put him on display in a blacking factory. At her best, Jane Austen wrote out of laughter. Her art came from the impish glee of a precocious teenager amused by the follies of the world around her, wanting to get us in on the joke. Her final voice is modulated, deepened, matured by life and its losses, but it is still the voice of the *Juvenalia*, the joyous voice of *Pride and Prejudice*, the voice of the narrator of *Emma* and of the comic passage in the unfinished *Sanditon*. It is the playful voice whose resonance is enriched by the piety that is always in, with, and under it. It is the voice of the supremely talented, supremely meticulous writer who lived and died as Jenny, whose greatness as a woman and as an artist is the greatness of one who became, and remained, a little child.

ACKNOWLEDGMENTS

This book has been a long time in coming. Originally commissioned for inclusion in the Cumberland Press Leaders In Action series, it was delayed when Cumberland Press went out of business in early 2009. I am grateful to David Vaughan and Cumberland Press for the challenge of participating in the initial series, and I am also grateful to Nelson for picking up the project.

I have taught Jane Austen's novels at New St. Andrews College on and off for a number of years, and I am thankful that the board and administration has been willing to give a theologian a chance to pontificate on literature. My students contributed a great deal to this book, particularly the students in my spring 2007 Austen elective. I assigned them Claire Tomalin's biography, and made them prepare oral presentations on chapters from that book. I tried to keep up the pretense that this assignment was in their own best interests, but I can now reveal that I was using them for free research assistance. Thanks to you all.

Several individuals deserve particular thanks. A former M.A. student, Brad Littlejohn, worked with the footnotes of an earlier draft, which shaped the book from rough-hewn to a semi-polished condition. My son, Christian, rearranged portions of the earlier manuscript as I prepared the book for a new publisher, and I could not have completed this project in a timely manner without his help. Finally, I am grateful to my literary agent, Aaron Rench, for his persistence and hard work in securing a new publisher when the original project was cancelled.

My initial work on this book was disrupted by my mother's illness and death during July 2007. Her literary sympathies were more with Louisa May Alcott than Jane Austen, and I don't know if she ever read a page of Austen. If she had, her response would have been mixed. She would have been bored by balls and flirtations, laughed at some of the characters, and frowned when she thought Jane's mockery stepped over the border into unkindness. For eighty-eight years, though, she embodied the Christian humility, selfless charity, childlike joy and playfulness that I believe were central to Austen's character and to her best characters. In that spirit, then, I dedicate this book to the memory of my mother, Mildred Carolyn (Woelke) Leithart.

ABOUT THE AUTHOR

[[to come]]

APPENDIX 1

AUSTEN'S FAMILY, FRIENDS,
AND NEIGHBORS

FAMILY:

Austen, Anne (Mathew): Jane Austen's sister-in-law; first wife of James Austen.

Austen, Caroline: Jane Austen's niece; daughter of her brother James and his second wife, Mary.

Austen, Cassandra (Leigh): Jane Austen's mother.

Austen, Cassandra: Jane Austen's only sister.

Austen, Charles: Jane Austen's only younger brother.

Austen, Francis: Jane Austen's great-uncle; uncle of her father, George.

Austen, Francis (Frank): Jane Austen's brother.

Austen, George: Jane Austen's father.

Austen, George: Jane Austen's invalid brother.

Austen, Henry: Jane Austen's favorite brother.

Austen, James: Jane Austen's oldest brother.

Austen, Martha (Lloyd): Jane Austen's sister-in-law, second wife to her brother Francis.

Austen, Mary (Gibson): Jane Austen's sister-in-law; first wife of her brother Francis.

Austen, Mary (Lloyd): Jane Austen's friend and sister-in-law; second wife of her brother James.

Austen, Rebecca Walter: Jane Austen's paternal grandmother.

Austen, William: Jane Austen's paternal grandfather.

Austen-Leigh, James Edward: Jane Austen's nephew; son of her brother James and his second wife, Mary.

Cooke, Cassandra: Jane Austen's mother's cousin, daughter of Thophilus Leigh II.

Cooper, Rev. E.: Jane Austen's uncle; brother-in-law to her mother.

Cooper, Rev. Edward: Jane Austen's cousin; son of her mother's sister Jane.

Cooper, Jane: Jane Austen's aunt; her mother's sister.

Cooper, Jane: Jane Austen's cousin; daughter of her mother's sister Jane.

de Feuillide, Comte Jean Capote: Married Jane Austen's cousin Eliza Hancock.

Hancock, Eliza: Jane Austen's cousin; daughter of her father's sister Philadelphia; married a French Comte, and later married Jane's brother Henry.

Hancock, Philadelphia (Austen): Jane Austen's aunt; sister of Jane's father.

Hancock, Tyson Saul: Jane Austen's uncle; brother-in-law to her father.

Knight, Edward Austen: Jane Austen's brother; adopted by the Knight family.

Knight, Elizabeth (Bridges): Jane Austen's sister-in-law; married to her brother Edward.

Knight, Fanny: Jane Austen's niece; daughter of her brother, Edward Knight.

Lefroy, Anna (Austen): Jane Austen's niece; daughter of her brother James and his first wife, Anne.

Leigh, Jane (Walker): Jane Austen's maternal grandmother.

Leigh, Mary: Jane Austen's mother's cousin; daughter of Theophilus Leigh II.

Leigh, Theophilus: Jane Austen's great-grandfather; her mother's grandfather.

Leigh, Theophilus II: Jane Austen's great-uncle; her mother's uncle.

Leigh, Thomas: Jane Austen's maternal grandfather.

Leigh, Thomas: Jane Austen's mentally disabled uncle; her mother's brother.

Leigh, Thomas: Cousin to Jane Austen's mother; resident of Stoneleigh Abbey.

Leigh-Perrot, James: Jane Austen's uncle; brother to her mother.

Leigh-Perrot, Jane (Cholmeley): Jane Austen's aunt; sister-in-law to her mother.

Perrot, Anne: Aunt to Jane Austen's uncle James Leigh-Perrot, her mother's brother.

Walter, Philadelphia (Phylly): Daughter of George Austen's half brother.

Walter, William Hampson: Jane Austen's father's half brother; son born to Rebecca Austen from her first marriage.

Friends, Neighbors, Acquaintances:

Bigg, Catherine: Childhood friend of Jane Austen; lived in Manydown Park.

Bigg, Elizabeth: Childhood friend of Jane Austen; lived in Manydown Park.

Bigg-Wither, Harris: Brother to Elizabeth and Catherine Bigg; proposed to Jane Austen in 1802.

Bigeon, Madame: Henry Austen's housekeeper, to whom Jane Austen left 50l at her death.

Blackall, Rev. Samuel: Madam Lefroy tried to match Jane with Rev. Blackall, but Jane was not interested.

Brydges, Samuel Egerson: Anne Lefroy's brother; a failed poet and later a successful novelist.

Burney, Fanny (also Madame d'Arblay): Popular writer of Austen's youth; neighbor to Jane's mother's cousin Catherine Cooke in Surrey.

Cawley, Mrs.: Jane Austen's teacher at a school in Oxford.

Chute, Tom: Childhood friend and occasional dance partner of Jane Austen, who lived at the Vyne.

Clarke, James Stanier: Librarian to the Prince Regent; offered Jane Austen unsolicited, and silly, literary advice.

Crosby, Benjamin: Owner of publishing house that promised to publish *Northanger Abbey*.

Dennis, Mrs. Ashton (MAD): Alias adopted by Jane Austen when she communicated with the Crosby publishing house.

Digweed, Harry: Childhood friend of Jane Austen; the Digweeds resided in the Steventon Manor House during Austen's childhood.

Egerton, Thomas: Owner of a London publishing house that published *Sense and Sensibility*.

Fowle, Fulwar: Pupil of Jane Austen's father; childhood friend of Jane.

Fowle, Fulwar William: Son of Fulwar Fowle.

Fowle, Rev. Thomas: Fiance of Jane Austen's sister Cassandra; he died in the West Indies before marriage.

Harwood, John: Childhood friend of Jane Austen; his family lived at Deane House.

Hastings, George: Son of Warren Hastings; died in childhood while in the care of Austen's parents.

APPENDIX 2

CHARACTERS IN AUSTEN'S NOVELS

Sense and Sensibility

Miss Steele
Doctor
Mrs. Norris
Uncle Philips
Robert Ferrars
Lady Middleton
Annamaria
Fanny Dashwood
Willoughby

Pride and Prejudice

Kitty Bennet
Mary Bennet
Elizabeth (Lizzie) Bennet
Jane Bennet
Mr Darcy
Mr Wickham
Lady Catherine
Mr Collins

Mansfield Park

William Price
Fanny Price
Henry Crawford
Mary Crawford

Emma

Mr Weston
Mr Woodhouse
Mr Knightley
Frank Churchill
Jane Fairfax
Emma Woodhouse
Mrs Elton
Mr Elton
Emma Woodhouse

Persuasion

Captain Wentworth
Admiral Croft
William Eliot
Mrs Clay

Northanger Abbey

Catherine Morland

NOTES

INTRODUCTION

1. Quoted in Deirdre Le Faye, *Jane Austen: A Family Record* (2d edition; Cambridge: CUP, 2004), 240–41.
2. Deidre Shauna Lynch, "Sequels," in Janet Todd, ed., *Jane Austen in Context* (Cambridge: CUP, 2005), 161.
3. When the production went to video, the entire stock of 12,000 sold out in two hours, and another 58,000 by the end of the week (Claire Harman, *Jane's Fame: How Jane Austen Conquered the World* [Edinburgh: Canongate, 2009], 256). Harman's last chapter is a brisk and up-to-date survey of what she calls Jane AustenTM.
4. Roger Sales, *Jane Austen and the Representations of Regency England* (London: Routledge, 1994), 17–25.
5. Harman, *Jane's Fame*, 275.
6. Ibid.
7. Ibid., 185.
8. Ibid., 217–18.
9. Harman (Ibid., 267) writes that "Once people are 'getting their Austen' from secondary or tertiary sources, there are no limits to what can become of her."
10. Quoted by Deidre Shauna Lynch, "Cult of Jane Austen," in Todd, ed., *Jane Austen*, 114.
11. Ibid., 114–17.
12. Chris Rojek, *Celebrity* (London: Reaktion Books, 2001).
13. Harman, *Jane's Fame*, 162.
14. Ibid., 165–66.
15. The term is Harman's, describing Austen in her later years.
16. Quoted in Le Faye, *Jane Austen*, 165.

CHAPTER 1: AUSTEN'S WORLD

1. Irene Collins, *Jane Austen: The Parson's Daughter* (London: Hambledon Press, 1998), 122.

2. Michael Wheeler, "Religion," in Janet Todd, ed., *Jane Austen in Context* (Cambridge: CUP, 2005), 407.

3. David Selwyn, "Consumer Goods," in Ibid., 217.

4. Deidre Le Faye, *Jane Austen: A Family Record* (2d edition; Cambridge: CUP, 2004), 20–21. The description of the sound as "scrooping" comes from Austen's nephew, James-Edward Austen Leigh. Also, Maggie Lane, *Jane Austen's England* (New York: St. Martin's, 1986), 37, 39.

5. Lane, *Jane Austen's England*, 39.

6. Ibid., 40.

7. Le Faye, *Jane Austen*, 13, 17.

8. J. E. Austen-Leigh, "A Memoir of Jane Austen" in Kathryn Sutherland, ed., *J. E. Austen-Leigh, A Memoir of Jane Austen and other Family Recollections* (Oxford World's Classics; Oxford: OUP, 2002), 10.

9. Le Faye, *Jane Austen*, 3.

10. Ibid., 5.

11. Ibid., 7, 22, 34–36.

12. See Henry Austen's description, quoted in Ibid., 44.

13. Ibid., 31.

14. Ibid., 6.

15. Ibid., 7, 13.

16. Collins, *Parson's Daughter*, 4.

17. Ibid., 6, 8.

18. David Cecil, *A Portrait of Jane Austen* (London: Penguin, 1980), 24.

19. Collins, *Parson's Daughter*, xix–xx.

20. Le Faye, *Jane Austen*, 17.

21. Collins, *Parson's Daughter*, 13.

22. Ibid. 45–46.

23. Henry Austen, "Memoir of Miss Austen," in Sutherland, *A Memoir*, 147.

24. Collins, *Parson's Daughter*, 59.

25. Deirdre Le Faye, ed., *Jane Austen's Letters* (new edition; Oxford:

OUP, 1997), Letter #78, 199. Hereafter, letters will be cited by letter number followed by the page number from the Le Faye edition.

26. Quoted in Cecil, *Portrait*, 33–34.

27. Quoted in Collins, *Parson's Daughter*, 48.

28. Quoted in Ibid., 45.

29. Le Faye, *Jane Austen*, 7.

30. Collins, *Parson's Daughter*, 21.

31. Ibid., 6. The examples of his wit are not overwhelming. One Mrs. Thrale wrote to Dr. Johnson of one incident in which Leigh was told that during a dispute among Privy Councillors, the Lord Chancellor struck the table. "No, no, no," replied the Theophilus, "I can hardly persuade myself that he split the table, though I believe he divided the Board." When Jane's brother James visited his venerable relative on his first trip to Oxford, he began to remove his robe for a meal, to which Theophilus responded: "Young man, you need not strip; we are not going to fight." Three days before his death: told of a friend who had become sick from eating eggs and then had married. Colleagues said he was "egged on to matrimony," to which Leigh retorted, "Then may the yoke sit easy on him" (J. E. Austen-Leigh, "A Memoir" in Sutherland, ed., *A Memoir*, 11–12).

32. Le Faye, *Jane Austen*, 10.

33. Quoted in Tomalin, *Jane Austen: A Life* (New York: Vintage, 1997), 27.

34. Claire Harman, *Jane's Fame: How Jane Austen Conquered the World* (Edinburgh: Canongate, 2009), 26–29.

35. Quoted in Collins, *Parson's Daughter*, 12.

36. Quoted in Ibid., 13.

37. Cecil, *Portrait*, 22.

38. Collins, *Parson's Daughter*, 8, 14.

39. Le Faye, *Jane Austen*, 84.

40. Ibid., 239.

41. Quoted in Ibid., 10.

42. Quoted in Collins, *Parson's Daughter*, 20.

43. Le Faye, *Jane Austen*, 8–9.

44. Caroline Austen, "My Aunt Jane Austen: A Memoir," in Sutherland, ed., *A Memoir*, 170.

45. David Selwyn, ed., The Complete Poems of James Austen: Jane Austen's Eldest Brother (Jane Austen Society, 2003), 55.

46. Harman, Jane's Fame, 85–86.

47. Ibid., 22–23.

48. Quoted in Le Faye, *Jane Austen*, 23.

49. So his mother thought; see Ibid., 53.

50. Ibid., 140.

51. Ibid., 48. He bought it for 1l 11s 6d, and sold it for a pound and shilling more.

52. Ibid., 125.

53. Ibid., 139–40.

54. Ibid., 26, 41.

55. Letter #63, 161.

56. Collins, *Parson's Daughter*, 201.

57. Ibid., 203.

58. Le Faye, *Jane Austen*, 235.

59. Ibid., 213.

60. Quoted in Ibid., 96.

61. The most complete account of Eliza's life is Deirdre Le Faye, *Jane Austen's 'Outlandish Cousin': The Life and Letters of Eliza de Feuillide* (London: British Library, 2002).

62. Caroline Austen, "My Aunt Jane Austen: A Memoir," in Sutherland, ed., *A Memoir*, 175.

63. Ibid.

64. Collins, *Parson's Daughter*, 48.

65. Ibid., 9.

66. Henry Austen, "A Memoir of Miss Austen," in Ibid., 153–54.

67. Edward Copeland, "Money," in Janet Todd, *Jane Austen in Context* (Cambridge: CUP, 2005), 317–26. Austen's novels present consumption items, luxury items, as markers of income and status, rather than merely presenting landed wealth and houses as a sign of wealth. A horse, a carriage, additional servants, a house in town—these extras signify the range of incomes among Austen's characters. Comparing purchasing power across the centuries is difficult. As Daniel Pool points out, "the fact that the Victorians had no Hondas and we have no candles, i.e., we don't buy the same goods and don't have the same economic needs, makes the purchasing power of the two currencies fundamentally

incommensurable. Nonetheless, intrepid estimates in the last ten years [Pool was writing in 1993] have put the pound's worth in the neighborhood of $20, $50, or $200." Darcy's annual income thus represents, in purchasing power, somewhere between $200,000 and $2,000,000 per year (Pool, *What Jane Austen Ate and Charles Dickens Knew: From Fox Hunting to Whist—the Facts of Daily Life in 19th-Century England* [New York: Simon and Schuster, 1994], 20–21).

68. Le Faye, *Jane Austen*, 18.

69. Collins, *Parson's Daughter*, 9.

70. Quoted in Ibid., 97.

71. Ibid., 98.

72. Le Faye, *Jane Austen*, 90, 182.

73. Cecil, *Portrait*, 41.

74. Ibid., 58.

75. Letter #15, 31.

76. Letter #39, 92–93.

77. Anna Lefroy, "Recollections of Aunt Jane," in Sutherland.

78. Collins, *Parson's Daughter*, 234.

79. Letter #151, 330.

80. Letter #12, 21.

81. Quoted in Collins, *Parson's Daughter*, 57.

CHAPTER 2: EDUCATION JENNY

1. Quoted in Irene Collins, *Jane Austen: The Parson's Daughter* (London: Hambledon, 1998), 33.

2. Ibid., 40.

3. Claire Tomalin, *Jane Austen: A Life* (London: Vintage, 1997), 44–45.

4. Quoted in Claire Harman, *Jane's Fame: How Jane Austen Conquered the World* (Edinburgh: Canongate, 2009), 15.

5. Le Faye, *Jane Austen: A Family Record* (2d ed.; Cambridge: CUP, 2004), 25–26.

6. Collins, *Parson's Daughter*, 26. A copy of *Goody Two-Shoes* with "Jane Austen" written on the front page still exists.

7. Quoted in Ibid., 28.

8. Anna Lefroy, in Kathryn Sutherland, ed., *J. E. Austen-Leigh, A*

Memoir of Jane Austen and Other Family Recollections (Oxford World's Classics; Oxford: OUP, 2002), 183. This comes from a letter to J. E. Austen-Leigh.

9. Le Faye, *Jane Austen*, 49, 57–58. C. S. Lewis, "A Note on Jane Austen," in Ian Watt, ed., *Jane Austen: A Collection of Critical Essays* (Englewood Cliffs, NJ: Prentice-Hall, 1963), 25–34.

10. Le Faye, *Jane Austen*, 50.

11. Collins, *Parson's Daughter*, 36.

12. Ibid., 65.

13. Harman, *Jane's Fame*, 34.

14. Collins, *Parson's Daughter*, 112.

15. Letter #63, 161.

16. Letter #17.

17. Caroline Austen, "My Aunt Jane Austen," in Sutherland, ed., *A Memoir*, 170.

18. Anna Lefroy, "Recollections," in Ibid., 182.

19. Letter #70, 181.

20. Letter #75, 194.

21. Letter #28, 65.

22. Letter #90, 229.

23. Le Faye, *Letters*, 455

24. David Cecil, *A Portrait of Jane Austen* (London: Penguin, 1980), 46–47.

25. Letter #26, 59.

26. Le Faye, *Jane Austen*, 114.

27. Ibid., 152.

28. Letter #146, 323.

29. Letter #145, 352.

30. Quoted in Harman, *Jane's Fame*, 56.

31. Collins, *Parson's Daughter*, 61–62.

32. Letter #14, 27.

33. Letter #50, 119.

34. Letter #89, 228.

35. William Deresiewicz, *Jane Austen and the Romantic Poets* (New York: Columbia University Press, 2005), 7.

36. Letter #9, 15.

37. Letter #14, 26.

38. Letter #1, 2.

39. Collins, *Parson's Daughter*, 62–63.
40. Caroline, "My Aunt Jane Austen," in Sutherland, ed., *A Memoir*, 174.
41. Le Faye, *Jane Austen*, 47, 59; Harman, *Jane's Fame*, 16.
42. Collins, *Parson's Daughter*, 107–08.
43. Ibid., 108.
44. Ibid., 114–18; cf. Letter #16.
45. Ibid, 125.
46. Ibid., 133.
47. Caroline, "My Aunt Jane Austen," in Sutherland, ed., *A Memoir*, 174.
48. Harman, *Jane's Fame*, 13.
49. Cecil, *Portrait*, 59.
50. Ibid., 60.
51. Ibid.
52. Harman, *Jane's Fame*, 25.
53. Jane Austen, *Catherine and Other Writings* (Margaret Anne Doody and Douglas Murray, eds.; Oxford World's Classics; Oxford: OUP, 1993), 135.
54. Austen, "Love and Freindship," in Ibid., 76.
55. Ibid., 78.
56. Austen, "The Beautiful Cassandra," in Ibid., 41–44.
57. Austen, "Sir William Montague," in Ibid., 38–39.
58. Quoted in Cecil, *Portrait*, 64.
59. Quoted in Le Faye, *Jane Austen*, 199.
60. Cecil, *Portrait*, 67.
61. Ibid., 65.
62. Ibid.

CHAPTER 3: EARLY MASTERPIECES

1. Irene Collins, *Jane Austen: The Parson's Daughter* (London: Hambledon Press, 1998), 112.
2. Ibid., 113.
3. Ibid., 113–15.
4. Ibid., 115.
5. Ibid., 131; Letters #5–6.
6. Letters #1–2

7. Quoted in Deirdre Le Faye, *Jane Austen: A Family Record* (2d ed.; Cambridge: CUP, 2004), 92.

8. Letter #1, 1.

9. Ibid., 2

10. Letter # 2, 4.

11. Ibid.

12. Collins, *Parson's Daughter*, 141.

13. Letter #11, 19.

14. Claire Tomalin, *Jane Austen: A Life* (New York: Vintage, 1997), 121.

15. Letter #11, 19.

16. Quoted in Le Faye, *Jane Austen*, 111.

17. Ibid., 100, 111.

18. Quoted in Cecil, *A Portrait of Jane Austen* (London: Penguin, 1980), 120.

19. Le Faye, *Jane Austen*, 73.

20. Collins, *Parson's Daughter*, 147–48.

21. www.jimandellen.org/austen/jachronology.writinglife.html.

22. Collins, *Parson's Daughter*, 195.

23. Ibid.

24. The characterization comes from Claire Harman, *Jane's Fame: How Jane Austen Conquered the World* (Edinburgh: Canongate, 2009).

25. Letter #109, 279–80.

26. Letter #114, 285–86.

27. Letter #82, 208.

28. Letter #153, 332.

29. Letter #151, 329.

30. I am following the interpretation offered by Julia Prewitt Brown, *Jane Austen's Novels: Social Change and Literary Form* (Cambridge, MA: Harvard, 1979), 156–70.

31. Letter #51, 124.

32. Letter #, 147–48

33. Letter #89, 225.

34. Ibid.

35. Letter #63, 159

36. Letter #67, 173.

37. Letter #30.

38. Gilbert Ryle, "Jane Austen and the Moralists," in B. C. Southam, *Critical Essays on Jane Austen* (London: Routledge, 1970), 117.

39. C. S. Lewis, "A Note on Jane Austen," in Ian Watt, ed., *Jane Austen: A Collection of Critical Essays* (Englewood Cliffs, NJ: Prentice-Hall, 1963).

40. Henry Austen, "A Memoir," in Sutherland, ed., *A Memoir*, 153.

41. G. D. Boyle in Ibid., 196. The quotation is from a letter to James Edward Austen-Leigh.

42. Letter #36, 84.

43. Letter #90, 231.

44. Letter #53, 131.

45. Collins, *Parson's Daughter*, 19.

46. Available at www.eskimo.com/~lhowell/bcp1662/baptism/catchism.html, accessed 7 August 2007.

47. Collins, *Parson's Daughter*, 49.

48. Available at www.pemberley.com/janeinfo/ausprayr.html.

Chapter 4: Disruptions

1. Letter #145, 320.

2. Letter #73, 188.

3. Letter #74, 191–92.

4. Letter #84, 210.

5. Letter #90, 230.

6. David Cecil, *A Portrait of Jane Austen* (London: Penguin, 1980), 90.

7. Caroline Austen, in Kathryn Sutherland, ed., *J. E. Austen-Leigh, A Memoir of Jane Austen and other Family Recollections* (Oxford World's Classics; Oxford: OUP, 2002), 185. This is from a letter to J. E. Austen-Leigh.

8. Irene Collins, *Jane Austen: The Parson's Daughter* (London: Hambledon Press, 1998), 220–23.

9. Ibid., 224–26.

10. Quoted in Maggie Lane, *Jane Austen's England* (New York: St. Martin's, 1986), 73.

11. Letter #35.

12. Quoted in Cecil, *Portrait*, 90.

13. Quoted in Ibid., 92.

14. Quoted in Ibid.
15. Deirdre Le Faye, *Jane Austen: A Family Record* (2d ed.; Cambridge: CUP, 2004), 136.
16. Letter from Caroline to James Edward Austen-Leight, in Sutherland, ed., *A Memoir*, 188.
17. Le Faye, *Jane Austen*, 117.
18. Letter from Catherine Hubback to James Edward Austen-Leigh, in Sutherland, ed., *A Memoir*, 191.
19. Cecil, *Portrait*, 98.
20. *Persuasion*.
21. Le Faye, *Jane Austen*, 145.
22. Letters #40–41, 95–98.
23. Quoted in Le Faye, *Jane Austen*, 146–47.
24. Harman, *Jane's Fame: How Jane Austen Conquered the World* (Edinburgh: Canongate, 2009), 42.
25. Ibid., 47–48.
26. Collins, *Parson's Daughter*, 232–33.
27. Quoted in Lane, *Jane Austen's England*, 143.
28. Le Faye, *Jane Austen*, 159.
29. Letter #35, 82; Letter #88, 223.
30. Letter #86, 217.
31. Letter #89, 224.
32. Collins, *Parson's Daughter*, 208.
33. Anna Lefroy, "Recollections," in Sutherland, ed., *A Memoir*, 158.
34. Cecil, *Portrait*, 112.
35. Quoted in Ibid., 112–13.
36. Ibid., 113.
37. Quoted in Cecil, *Portrait*, 128.
38. Caroline Austen, "My Aunt Jane Austen," in Sutherland, ed., *A Memoir*, 171.
39. Ibid.
40. Harman, Jane's Fame, 66.
41. *Sense and Sensibility*, chapter 21.
42. Letter #53, 129.
43. Letter #94, 234.
44. Letter #71, 182.
45. Letter #5, 140.
46. Letter #88, 223.

47. Le Faye, *Letters*, 578.
48. http://www.pemberley.com/janeinfo/ausetpm.html   Accessed September 25, 2009.
49. Anna Lefroy, "Recollections of Aunt Jane," in Sutherland, ed., *A Memoir*, 157–58.
50. Caroline Austen, "My Aunt Jane Austen," in Ibid., 169.
51. Ibid., 169.
52. Ibid., 171.
53. Quoted in Le Faye, *Jane Austen*, 149–50.
54. Letter #50, 120.
55. Letter #45, 107.
56. Caroline, "My Aunt Jane Austen," in Sutherland, ed., *A Memoir*, 175.
57. J. E. Austen-Leigh, "A Memoir of Jane Austen," in Ibid., 10.
58. Letter #60, 150.
59. Letter #62, 157.
60. Letter #87, 219.
61. Letter #84, 211.
62. Letter #80, 203.
63. Letter #82, 208.
64. Letter #78, 198.
65. Letter #15, 29.
66. Letter #27, 61.
67. Le Faye, *Jane Austen*, 202.
68. Anna Lefroy, "Recollections," in Sutherland, ed., *A Memoir*, 159.
69. Letter #85, 212.
70. Letter #146, 322–23.
71. Letter #146, 322.
72. Letter #148, 324.
73. Collins, *Parson's Daughter*, 206.
74. Letter #87.

Chapter 5: Published Author

1. Letter #37, 86.
2. Claire Harman, *Jane's Fame: How Jane Austen Conquered the World* (Edinburgh: Canongate, 2009), is particularly good on Austen's literary ambitions and desire to be paid for her work,

though she sometimes takes Austen's more than half-joking references to ambition and greed too straightforwardly.

3. Ibid., 38.
4. Ibid., 270–71.
5. Quoted in Ibid., 46.
6. Maggie Lane, *Jane Austen's England* (London: St. Martin's, 1986), 156.
7. Cecil, Portrait, 156
8. Letter #80, 203.
9. Letter #79, 101.
10. Letter #80, 203.
11. Letter #80, 203.
12. Letter #2, 3.
13. Letter #32, 74–75.
14. Letter #66, 170.
15. David Cecil, *A Portrait of Jane Austen* (London: Penguin, 1980), 156.
16. Ibid.
17. Ibid., 162.
18. Letter #90, 231.
19. Henry Austen, "Memoir of Miss Austen" in Kathryn Sutherland, ed., J. E. Austen-Leigh, *A Memoir of Jane Austen and other Family Recollections* (Oxford World's Classics; Oxford: OUP, 2002), 149.
20. Henry Austen, "A Memoir," in Sutherland, ed., *A Memoir*, 150
21. Letter #65, 168.
22. Letter #90, 231.
23. Letter #62, 156.
24. Letter #22, 47.
25. Letter #21, 42.
26. Letter #25, 55.
27. Letter #138D, 312.
28. Letter #104, 269.
29. Letter #107, 274–75.
30. Letter #108, 277
31. Letter #146, 323.
32. Irene Collins, *Jane Austen: The Parson's Daughter* (London: Hambledon Press, 1998), 126.
33. Ibid., 150.

34. Quoted in Deirdre Le Faye, *Jane Austen: A Family Record* (2d ed.; Cambridge: CUP, 2004), 230.
35. Letter #62.
36. Letter #153.
37. Description from Le Faye, *Jane Austen*, 225.
38. Letter #125, 296–97.
39. Letter #132A, 307.
40. Letter #132, 306.
41. Letter #138A, 311.
42. Letter #138D, 312.
43. Quoted in Harman, *Jane's Fame*, 71.
44. Letter #125D, 296.
45. Letter #125A, 296.
46. Caroline Austen, "My Aunt Jane Austen," in Sutherland, ed., *A Memoir*, 176.
47. Letter #126, 297.
48. Letter #127, 298.
49. Letter #121, 291.
50. Letter #132D, 306.
51. Letter #56, 140.
52. Letter #49, 117.
53. Letter #39, 94.
54. Letter #90, 231–32.
55. Letter #94, 246.
56. Letter #113, 384–85.
57. Letter #94, 246.
58. Letter #152, 328–30.
59. Letter #153, 334.
60. Letter CEA/3, 347
61. Forster, *Aspects of the Novel* (London: Edwin Arnold, 1927), 75–76.
62. Gilbert Ryle, Review of W. A. Craik, *Jane Austen: The Six Novels* in *The Review of English Studies*, New Series, 17, 178 (August 1966), 337.

CHAPTER 6: DEATH

1. Henry Austen, "A Memoir of Miss Austen," in Kathryn Sutherland,

ed., J. E. Austen-Leigh, *A Memoir of Jane Austen and other Family Recollections* (Oxford World's Classics; Oxford: OUP, 2002), 150–51.

2. Letter #157, 338–39.
3. Letter #153, 331–32.
4. Letter #142, 316.
5. Henry Austen, "Memoir," in Sutherland, ed., *A Memoir*, 147.
6. Caroline Austen, "My Aunt Jane Austen," in Ibid., 178–79.
7. Ibid., 181.
8. Quoted in Deirdre Le Faye, *Jane Austen: A Family Record* (2d ed.; Cambridge: CUP, 2004), 251–52.
9. Quoted in Ibid., 252.
10. Quoted in Ibid., 251.
11. Letter #158, 339.
12. Letter #CEA/2, 346.
13. Letter #43, 100.
14. Letter #58, 147.
15. Letter #140, 313.
16. Letter #10, 17.
17. Letter #37, 88.
18. Letter #38, 90.
19. Letter #74, 191.
20. Letter #59, 147.
21. Letter #8, 13.
22. Letter #58, 146
23. Letter #67, 173.
24. Collins, *Parson's Daughter*, 124.
25. Letter #106, 273.
26. Letter #159, 340–41.
27. Letter #161, 343.
28. Le Faye, *Jane Austen*, 253.
29. Available at http://famouspoetsandpoems.com/poets/jane_austen/poems/3469.
30. Quoted in Le Faye, *Jane Austen*, 253.
31. Letter CEA/1, 344.
32. Le Faye, *Jane Austen*, 256.
33. Anna Lefroy, "Recollections," in Sutherland, ed., *A Memoir*, 159.

CHAPTER 7: FROM DIVINE JANE BACK TO JENNY

1. Quoted in Claire Tomalin, *Jane Austen: A Life* (New York: Vintage, 1997), 221.
2. Quoted in Ibid., 220.
3. Quoted in Ibid., 221. See Mary Waldron, "Critical responses, early," in Janet Todd, ed., *Jane Austen in Context* (Cambridge: CUP, 2005), 83–91.
4. David Cecil, *A Portrait of Jane Austen* (London: Penguin, 1980), 181.
5. Letter #139, 313.
6. Waldron, "Critical Responses," 89–90.
7. http://www.pemberley.com/janeinfo/janeart.html
   Accessed September 25, 2009
8. Available at www.pemberley.com/janeinfo/janeart.html#swscott2.
9. J. E. Austen-Leigh, "A Memoir of Jane Austen" in Kathryn Sutherland, ed., *J. E. Austen-Leigh, A Memoir of Jane Austen and Other Family Recollections* (Oxford World's Classics; Oxford: OUP, 2002), 104.
10. Ibid., 104.
11. Quoted in Claudia Johnson, "Austen cults and cultures," in Edward Copeland and Juliet McMaster, eds., *The Cambridge Companion to Jane Austen* (Cambridge: CUP, 1997), 211.
12. Nicola Trott, "Critical Responses, 1830–1970," in Todd, ed., *Jane Austen*, 92–92.
13. Norbert Elias, *The Civilizing Process: Sociogenesis and Psychogenetic Investigations* (rev. ed.; trans. Edmund Jephcott; ed. Eric Dunning, Johan Goudsblom, and Stephen Mennell; Oxford: Blackwell, 2000), p. ix.
14. Available at whitewolf.newcastle.edu.au/words/authors/K/Kipling Rudyard/prose/DebtsandCredits/janeites.html.
15. From "Jane Austen" in *A Common Reader*, available at etext. library.adelaide.edu.au/w/woolf/virginia/w91c/chapter12.html.

APPENDIX 3

1. The following genealogical charts are taken from http://www. pemberley.com/janeinfo/brabletn.html, which compiles its information from James Edward Austen-Leigh's memoir as well as Deirdre Le Faye's *Jane Austen: A Family Record*.